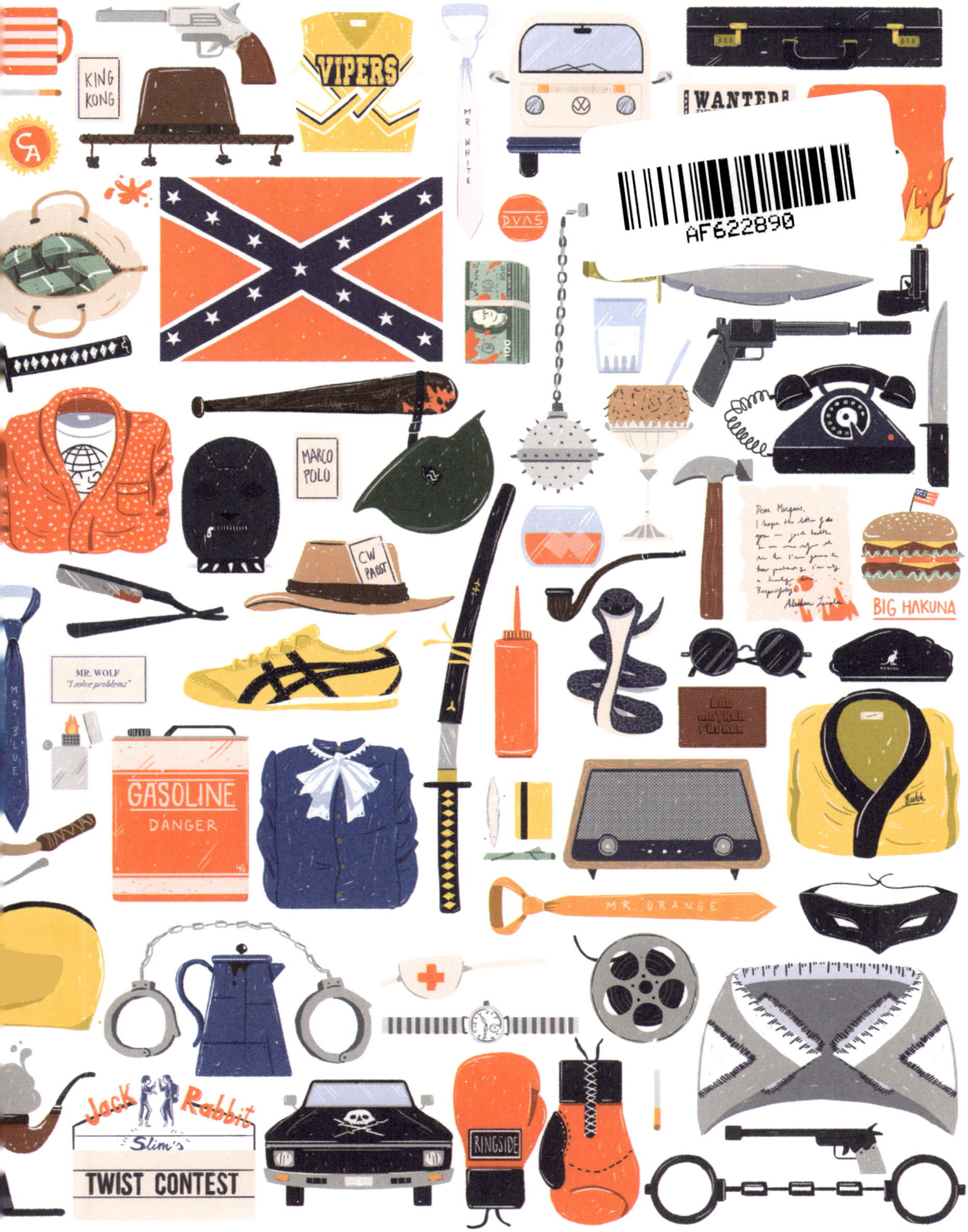
KING KONG
VIPERS
MR WHITE
WANTED
DVAS
MARCO POLO
CW PABST
MR. WOLF
"I solve problems"
MR BLUE
GASOLINE
DANGER
BIG HAKUNA
BAD MOTHER FUCKER
MR. ORANGE
Jack Rabbit
Slim's
TWIST CONTEST
RINGSIDE

TARANTINO

TARANTINO

- Tribute -

First edition in 2019 by Monsa Publications,
Gravina 43 (08930) Sant Adrià de Besós.
Barcelona (Spain) T +34 93 381 00 50
www.monsa.com monsa@monsa.com

Editor and Project Director Anna Minguet
Author, Art Director & Layout Eva Minguet
(Monsa Publications)
©The images belong to the authors
Cover image www.julianrentzsch.de &
www.stellavie.com
Back cover Joshua Budich
www.joshuabudich.com
Printed by Cachiman Grafic

Shop online:
www.monsashop.com

Follow us!
Instagram: @monsapublications
Facebook: @monsashop

ISBN: 978-84-17557-05-8
D.L. B 16176-2019

TARANTINO

- Tribute -

By Eva Minguet

monsa

INTRO

Quentin Tarantino is one of the leading filmmaker's of the 90s, known for his unique scenes, exquisite soundtracks, violence and coarse language. He gave the cinematographic montage format a new twist, presenting his stories with no chronological order from beginning to end. Tarantino pays tributes in each of his films and creates unique situations in which the grotesque can become amusing, even causing you to laugh.
The filmmaker also has many loyal collaborators including Samuel L. Jackson, Tim Roth, Uma Thurman, Michael Madsen, Harvey Keitel, Zoë Bell, Christoph Waltz, Leonardo DiCaprio, Brad Pitt... there are few actors who do not repeat the experience of working under Tarantino's direction, and this is not only pleasing to the director, but also highly appreciated by the audience.
This book is a tribute to Quentin Tarantino and the whole universe he has created. Here, you will see different fan art works by 32 international artists, authentic masterpieces, accompanied by phrases and anecdotes from the world of this fantastic filmmaker.

If you are one of the few who has not yet seen Tarantino's films, just sit back on the sofa and enjoy the work of this genius.

Quentin Tarantino es un cineasta referente de los 90, por sus escenas únicas, sus exquisitas bandas sonoras, la violencia y lenguaje vulgar de sus diálogos llenos de ironía. Renovó la fórmula del montaje cinematográfico, dejando ver sus historias sin un orden cronológico de principio a fin. Tarantino realiza homenajes en cada una de sus películas y crea situaciones en las que lo grotesco puede llegar a ser divertido, incluso provocando algunas carcajadas.
El cineasta también cuenta con fieles colaboradores entre los que se encuentran Samuel L. Jackson, Tim Roth, Uma Thurman, Michael Madsen, Harvey Keitel, Zoë Bell, Christoph Waltz, Leonardo DiCaprio, Brad Pitt... pocos son los actores que no repiten experiencia bajo el mando de Tarantino, y esto no sólo gusta al director, sino que también es muy valorado por los espectadores.
Este es un libro tributo a Quentin Tarantino y a todo el universo que ha creado. A continuación, veréis diferentes trabajos de fan art de 32 artistas internacionales, auténticas obras de arte, que irán acompañadas de frases y anécdotas del mundo de este fantástico cineasta.

Si eres de los pocos que aún no ha visto la filmografía de Tarantino, siéntate en el sofá, y disfruta del trabajo de este genio.

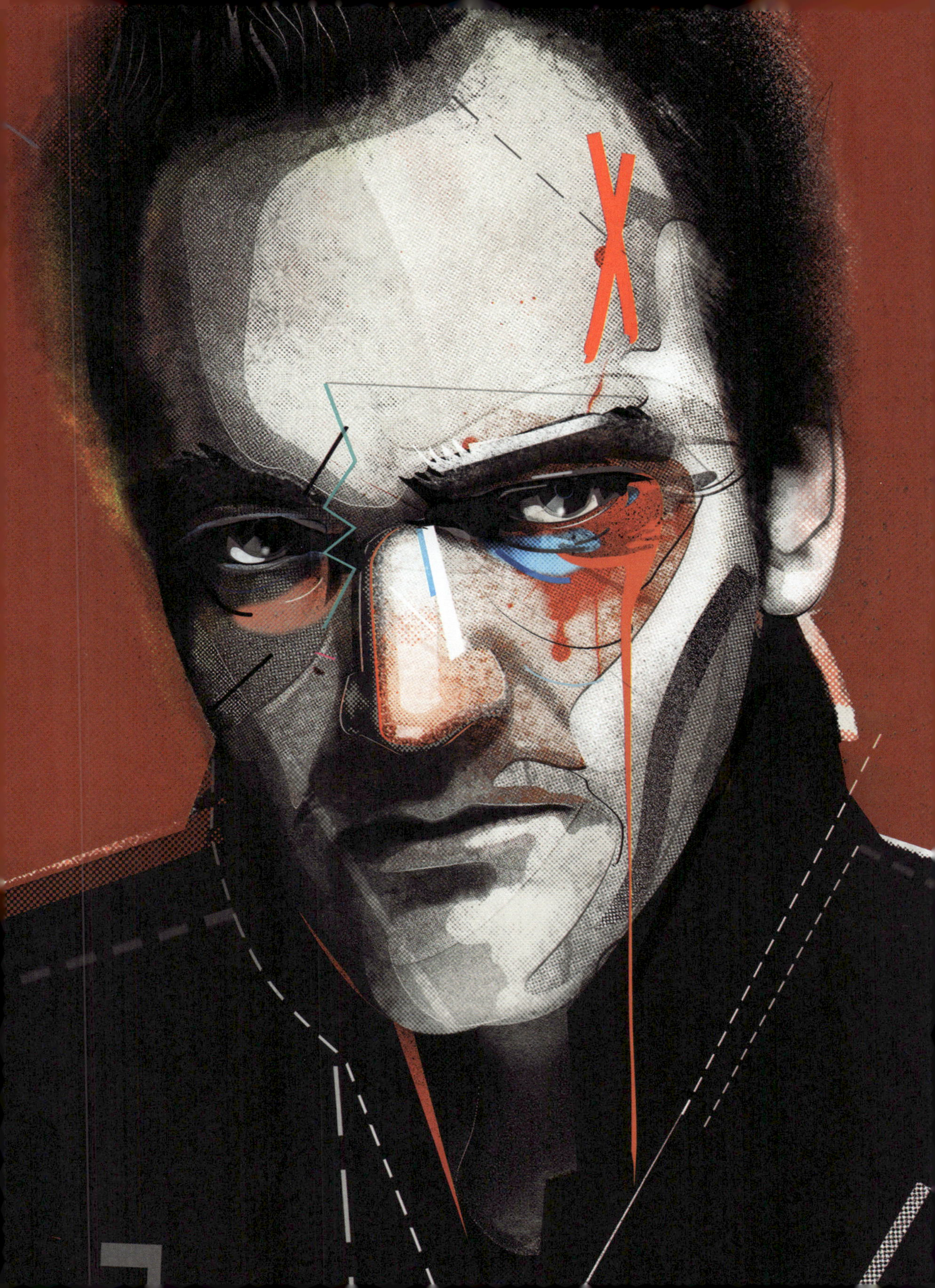

1992 RESERVOIR DOGS

Six professional criminals are hired to rob a diamond store, but the police appear unexpectedly at the time of the robbery. Some gang members die in the clash and others manage to get away, regrouping in a warehouse and preparing to find out who blew the whistle on them.

Seis criminales profesionales son contratados para robar en un almacén de diamantes, pero la policía aparece inesperadamente en el momento del atraco. Algunos miembros de la banda mueren en el enfrentamiento y otros logran huir, reagrupándose en un almacén y dispuestos a descubrir quién los delató.

1994 PULP FICTION

Vincent Vega and Jules Winnfield are two hitmen who work for Marsellus Wallace. After instructing them to recover a valuable briefcase, Marsellus orders Vincent to take care of Mia (his girlfriend) while he is out of town. Jules recommends him to be careful because it is very dangerous to overstep the mark with the boss's girlfriend. At the same time, the boxer Butch Coolidge tries to escape from the city after not going through with the rigged fight he had planned with Wallace, who decides he must die for his betrayal. The three stories intertwine to close a circle as original as it is unpredictable.

Vincent Vega y Jules Winnfield son dos asesinos a sueldo que trabajan para Marsellus Wallace. Tras encargarles que recuperen un valioso maletín, Marsellus le ordena a Vincent que se haga cargo de Mia (su novia) mientras él está fuera de la ciudad. Jules le recomienda prudencia porque es muy peligroso sobrepasarse con la novia del jefe. Paralelamente, el boxeador Butch Coolidge pretende escapar de la ciudad tras no cumplir con el combate amañado que había acordado con Wallace, y éste decide que debe morir. Las tres historias irán entrelazándose hasta cerrar un círculo tan original como imprevisible.

1997 JACKIE BROWN

Arms dealer Ordell Robbie uses the services of Jackie Brown, an air hostess who needs money and acts as a courier to bring him, little by little, the half a million dollars he keeps in Cabo San Luis, Mexico.

Everything seems to be going well until one day she is apprehended at customs and accused of drug trafficking by police officers Mark Dagus and Ray Nicolette. She will only be able to avoid prison if she accepts a proposal from the police: help them nab Robbie.

Ordell Robbie, traficante de armas utiliza los servicios de Jackie Brown, una azafata de vuelo que necesita dinero y hace de correo para traer poco a poco el medio millón de dólares que guarda en Cabo San Luis, México.

Todo parece ir bien hasta que un día es sorprendida en la aduana y acusada de tráfico de drogas por los policías Mark Dagus y Ray Nicolette. Sólo podrá evitar su ingreso en prisión, si acepta una propuesta de la policía: ayudarles a llegar hasta Robbie.

2003
2004

KILL BILL I - II

Volume 1: A pregnant woman is assaulted and given up for dead on the day of her wedding rehearsal. The culprits are her former comrades of the Lethal Viper Killer Squad, a group of professional killers working under Bill's command.
After waking up from a deep coma and realising she has lost the baby she was expecting, she embarks on a journey in which she will take revenge on her partners, her first targets being Vernita Green and O-Ren Ishii, leader of the gang of 88 Maniacs, and the lethal Gogo Yubari.

Volume 2: After doing away with some of the members of the gang that tried to murder her on her wedding day, "Black Mamba" continues her revenge and tries to kill the rest of the gang, especially their leader and former boss, Bill.

Volumen 1: Una mujer embarazada es agredida y dada por muerta en el día del ensayo de su boda. Los culpables son sus antiguos camaradas del Escuadrón Asesino Víbora Letal, un grupo de asesinos profesionales que trabajan bajo el mando de Bill.
Tras despertar de un coma profundo y darse cuenta de que ha perdido el bebé que esperaba, se embarca en un viaje en el que se vengará de sus socios, los primeros objetivos serán Vernita Green y O-Ren Ishii líder de la banda de los 88 Maníacos y la letal Gogo Yubari.

Volumen 2: Tras eliminar a algunos de los miembros de la banda que intentó asesinarla el día de su boda, "Mamba negra" continúa con su venganza e intenta acabar con el resto de la banda, en especial con su líder y antiguo jefe, Bill.

2007

DEATH PROOF

It is part of Grindhouse along with Robert Rodriguez's Planet Terror. The film revolves around a highway psychopath named Stuntman Mike, a serial killer who travels the highways to annihilate his victims with his "death-proof" car and quench his thirst for blood.

Forma parte de Grindhouse junto con Planet Terror de Robert Rodriguez. La película gira en torno a un psicópata de la carretera llamado Especialista Mike un asesino en serie que va recorriendo las carreteras para aniquilar a sus víctimas, con su coche "a prueba de muerte" y saciar su sed de sangre.

2009

INGLORIOUS BASTERDS

During World War II (1939-1945) France is occupied by the Germans. Shosanna Dreyfus witnesses the execution of her family by Nazi colonel Hans Landa. Shosanna manages to escape and flees to Paris, taking on a new identity as a cinema owner. Elsewhere in Europe, Lieutenant Aldo Raine organises a group of Jewish soldiers known to the enemy as "The Basterds". They will carry out a mission that will bring down the bosses of the Third Reich. As fate would have it, they all come together in a cinema, where Shosanna awaits her chance for revenge.

Durante la Segunda Guerra Mundial (1939-1945) Francia es ocupada por los alemanes. Shosanna Dreyfus presencia la ejecución de su familia a manos del coronel nazi Hans Landa. Shosanna consigue escapar y huye a París, adoptando una nueva identidad como propietaria de un cine. En otro lugar de Europa, el teniente Aldo Raine organiza un grupo de soldados judíos conocidos por el enemigo como "The Basterds". Llevarán a cabo una misión que hará caer a los jefes del Tercer Reich. El destino quiere que todos se encuentren en el interior del cine donde Shosanna espera para vengarse.

2012

DJANGO UNCHAINED

In Texas, two years before the outbreak of the American Civil War, King Schultz, a German bounty hunter on the trail of some murderers, releases a black slave named Django, promising to give him his freedom if he helps him catch the killers known as the Brittle Brothers. He accepts, as he later wants to go and find his wife Broomhilda, slave of the landowner Calvin Candie.

En Texas, dos años antes de estallar la Guerra Civil Americana, King Schultz un cazarrecompensas alemán, que va tras la pista de unos asesinos, libera a un esclavo negro llamado Django, con la promesa de dejarlo en libertad si le ayuda a atrapar a unos asesinos conocidos como los hermanos Brittle. Él acepta, pues luego quiere ir a buscar a su esposa Broomhilda, esclava del terrateniente Calvin Candie.

2015

THE HATEFUL EIGHT

Inside a stagecoach we find bounty hunter John Ruth and his trapped fugitive Daisy Domergue. He is trying to get quickly to the town of Red Rock, where she is to be hanged. Along the way, they meet two strangers: Major Marquis Warren and Chris Mannix, Red Rock's new sheriff. To take refuge from a blizzard they decide to stop at Minnie's Haberdashery, a shelter equipped for stagecoaches. When they arrive there, they are not received by the owner, but by four unknown faces. Bob, the new person in charge of the place, Oswaldo Mobray, Red Rock's executioner, the cowboy Joe Gage and the confederate general Sanford Smithers.

Encontramos en el interior de una diligencia al cazarrecompensas John Ruth y su fugitiva Daisy Domergue, que intentan llegar rápidamente al pueblo de Red Rock, donde ella será ejecutada en la horca. Por el camino, se encuentran con dos desconocidos: el mayor Marquis Warren y Chris Mannix, el nuevo sheriff de Red Rock. Para refugiarse de una ventisca deciden parar en la Mercería de Minnie, un refugio equipado para diligencias. Al llegar al lugar, no son recibidos por su dueña, sino por cuatro rostros desconocidos. Bob, el nuevo responsable del local, Oswaldo Mobray, verdugo de Red Rock, el vaquero Joe Gage y el general confederado Sanford Smithers.

2019

ONCE UPON A TIME IN HOLLYWOOD

In the late 1960s in Hollywood, we find the first changes in the film industry. Rick Dalton, a former TV Western star, tries to adapt to these changes at the same time as his life-long stuntman, Cliff Booth. As Rick sees his career come to an end, actress and model Sharon Tate will come into their lives unexpectedly.

Finales de los años 60 en Hollywood, encontramos los primeros cambios de la industria. Rick Dalton, una antigua estrella de Western televisivo, intenta amoldarse a estos cambios al mismo tiempo que su doble de acción de toda la vida, Cliff Booth. Mientras Rick ve el final de su carrera, la actriz y modelo Sharon Tate entra en sus vidas de forma inesperada.

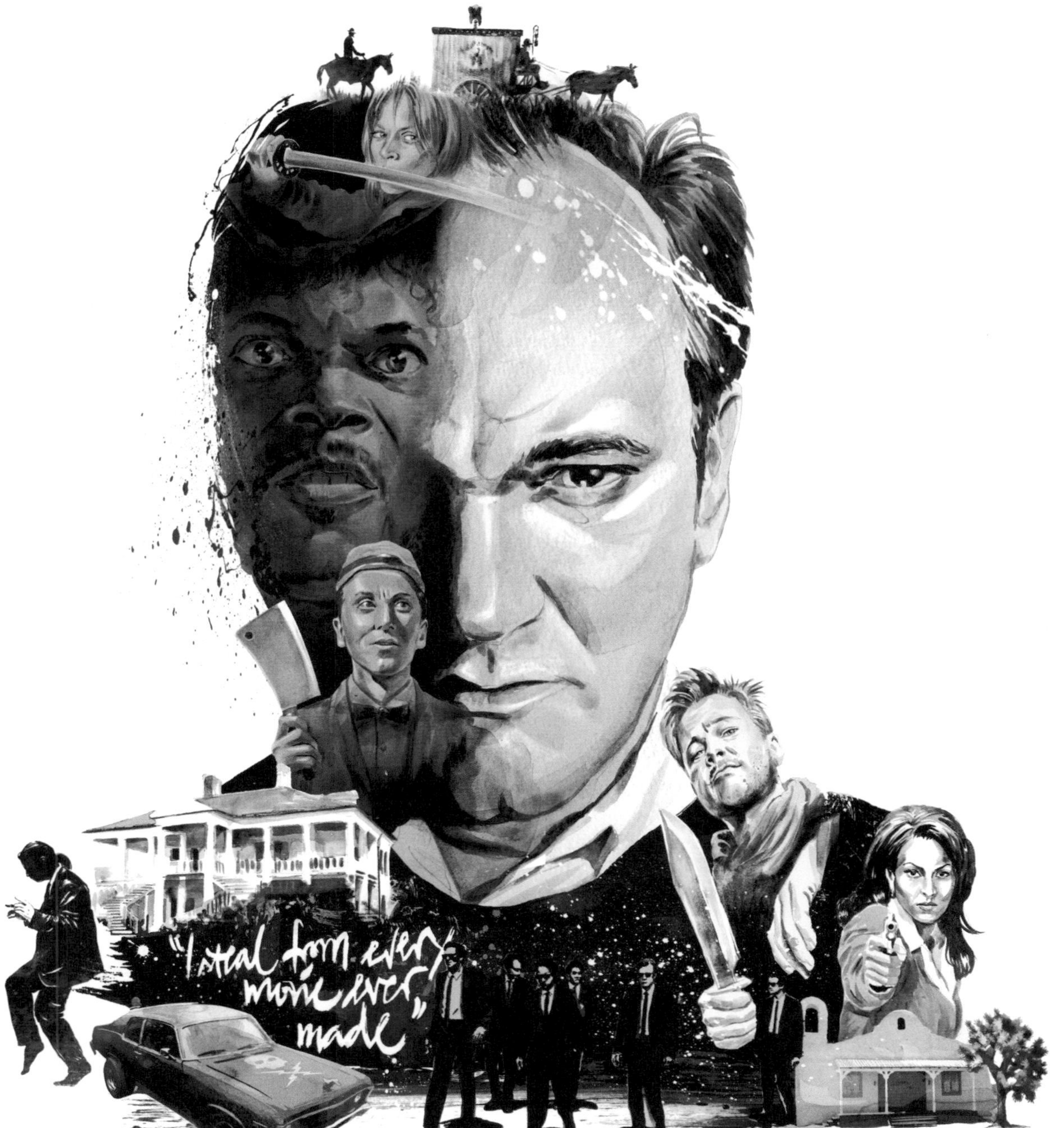

BIRTH NAME QUENTIN JEROME TARANTINO BORN MARCH 27, 1963, KNOXVILLE, TENNESSEE, US OCCUPATION DIRECTOR, PRODUCER, ACTOR, SCREENWRITER YEARS ACTIVE 1987—PRESENT

FAMOUS FOR RESERVOIR DOGS (1992) TRUE ROMANCE (1993) PULP FICTION (1994) NATURAL BORN KILLERS (1994) FROM DUSK TILL DAWN (1996) JACKIE BROWN (1997) KILL BILL: VOL. 1 (2003) KILL BILL: VOL. 2 (2004) CSI VEGAS — GRAVE DANGER (2005) DEATH PROOF (2007) INGLOURIOUS BASTERDS (2009) DJANGO UNCHAINED (2012) THE HATEFUL EIGHT (2015)

RECURRING ACTORS TIM ROTH, HARVEY KEITEL, MICHAEL MADSEN, STEVE BUSCEMI, UMA THURMAN, SAMUEL L. JACKSON, BRUCE WILLIS, CHRISTOPHER WALKEN, CHRISTOPH WALTZ, TARANTINO HIMSELF

TRIVIA THE BIG KAHUNA (BURGER) IS MENTIONED IN SEVERAL OF TARANTINOS FILMS FIRST SCREENPLAY CAPTAIN PEACHFUZZ AND THE ANCHOVY BANDIT (AT AGE 22)

RECEIVED BEST ORIGINAL SCREENPLAY OSCAR PULP FICTION (1994) DJANGO UNCHAINED (2012)

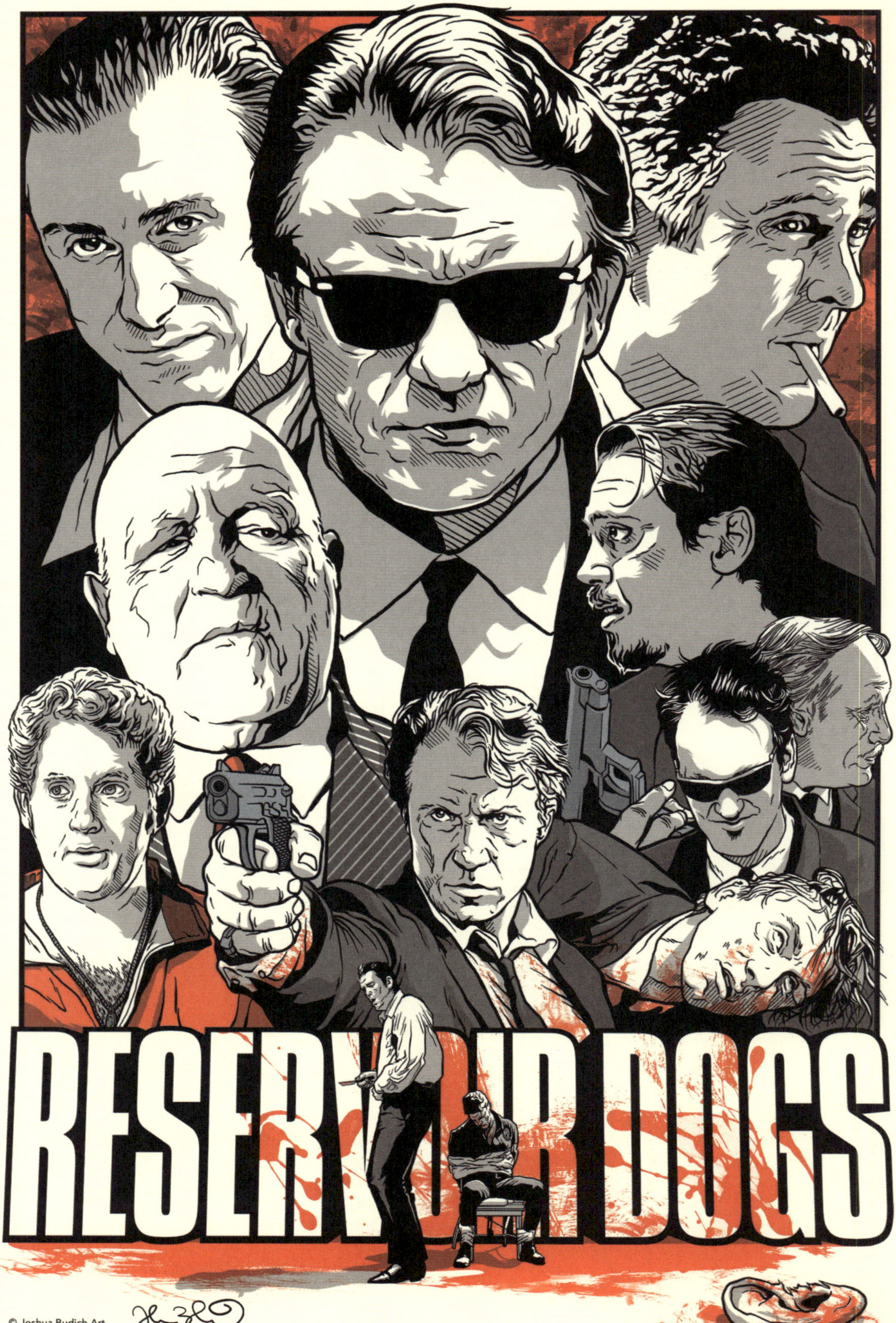
RESERVOIR DOGS

RESERVOIR DOGS

1992

Premiere

On 21 January 1992, the Sundance Film Festival hosted the world premiere of 'Reservoir Dogs', Quentin Tarantino's stunning debut feature. One of the hallmarks of his cinema are the references to films that had an impact on him in his youth. A clear example in Reservoir Dogs is the case of the code names assigned to the members of the gang, which pay tribute to the film Pelham 1.2.3. directed by Joseph Sargent in 1974, in which a group of criminals use colours as a code while they hijack an underground carriage in New York City.

El 21 de enero de 1992, el Festival de Sundance acogió la premiere mundial de 'Reservoir Dogs', la impactante ópera prima de Quentin Tarantino. Una de las peculiaridades de su cine, son los guiños y referencias a películas que le marcaron en su juventud. Un claro ejemplo en Reservoir Dogs es el caso de los nombres clave asignados a los miembros de la banda, que homenajea a la película Pelham 1.2.3. dirigida en 1974 por Joseph Sargent, en la cual un grupo de delincuentes usan colores como clave mientras secuestran un vagón de metro en la ciudad de Nueva York.

Mr. Orange

His real name is Freddy Newandyke, a police informer who has infiltrated the gang to capture Joe Cabot. After being shot during the escape, he tries to survive while bleeding to death, which helps him build his trust with Mr. White, who continues to defend him until the end, despite the conflicting opinion of the rest of the gang.

Su verdadero nombre es Freddy Newandyke, un informante de la policía que se ha infiltrado en la banda para capturar a Joe Cabot. Tras recibir un disparo durante la huida, intenta sobrevivir mientras se desangra, esto le ayudará a aumentar su confianza con el Sr. Blanco, que sigue defendiéndole hasta el final, pese a la opinión contraria del resto de la banda.

Mr. White

A middle-aged and very experienced thief. His real name is Larry Dimick. He and Joe Cabot have been working together for many years. He's used to killing, but he doesn't do it without a reason. He seems like the archetype of the honest criminal, with honour and principles. For him, feelings are more important than reason, which is why he stands up to his boss to defend Mr. Orange's honour, with fatal consequences for everyone.

Un ladrón de mediana edad y con mucha experiencia. Su verdadero nombre es Larry Dimick. Joe Cabot y él llevan muchos años trabajando juntos. Está acostumbrado a matar, pero no lo hace sin motivo. Parece el arquetipo del criminal honesto, con honor y principios. Para él los sentimientos valen más que la razón, causa por la que defiende el honor del Sr. Naranja ante su jefe, llegando a un final fatídico para todos.

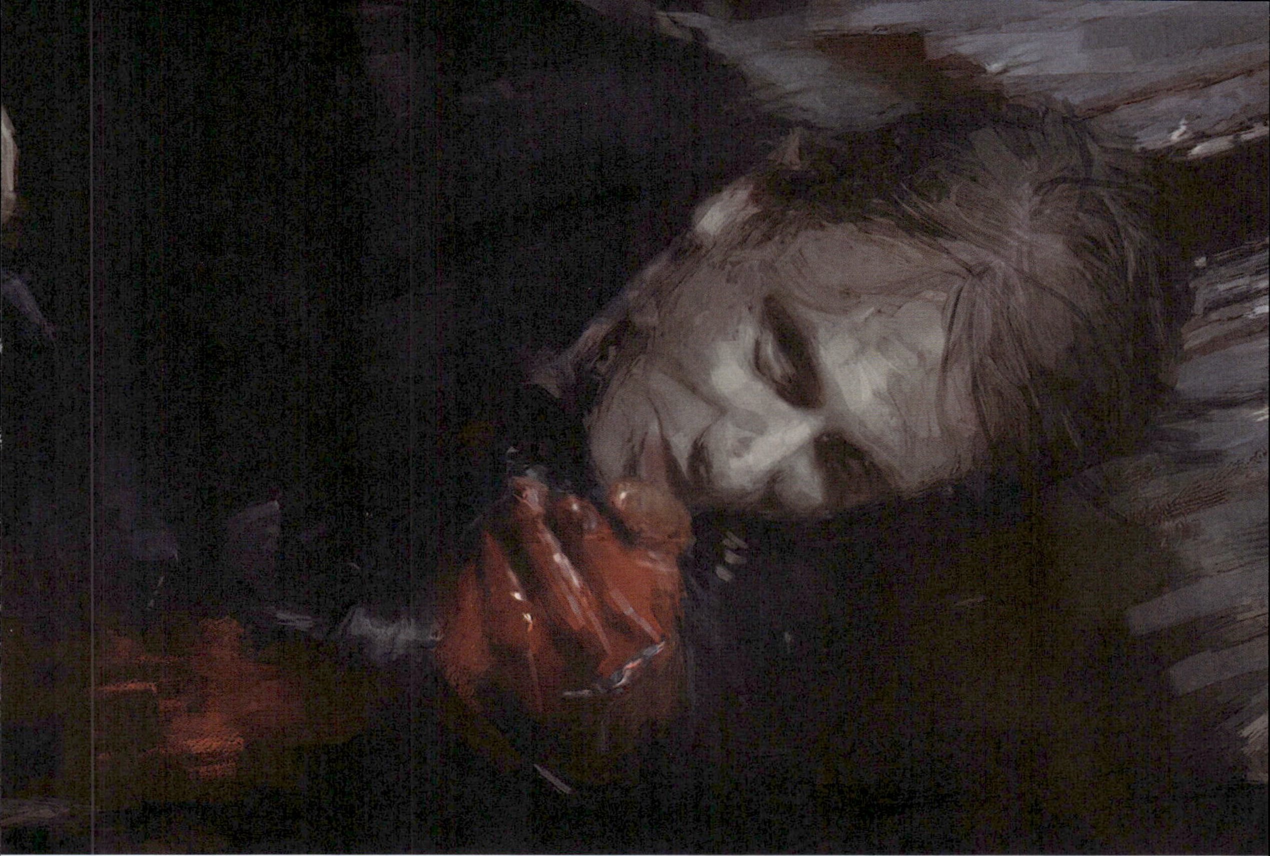

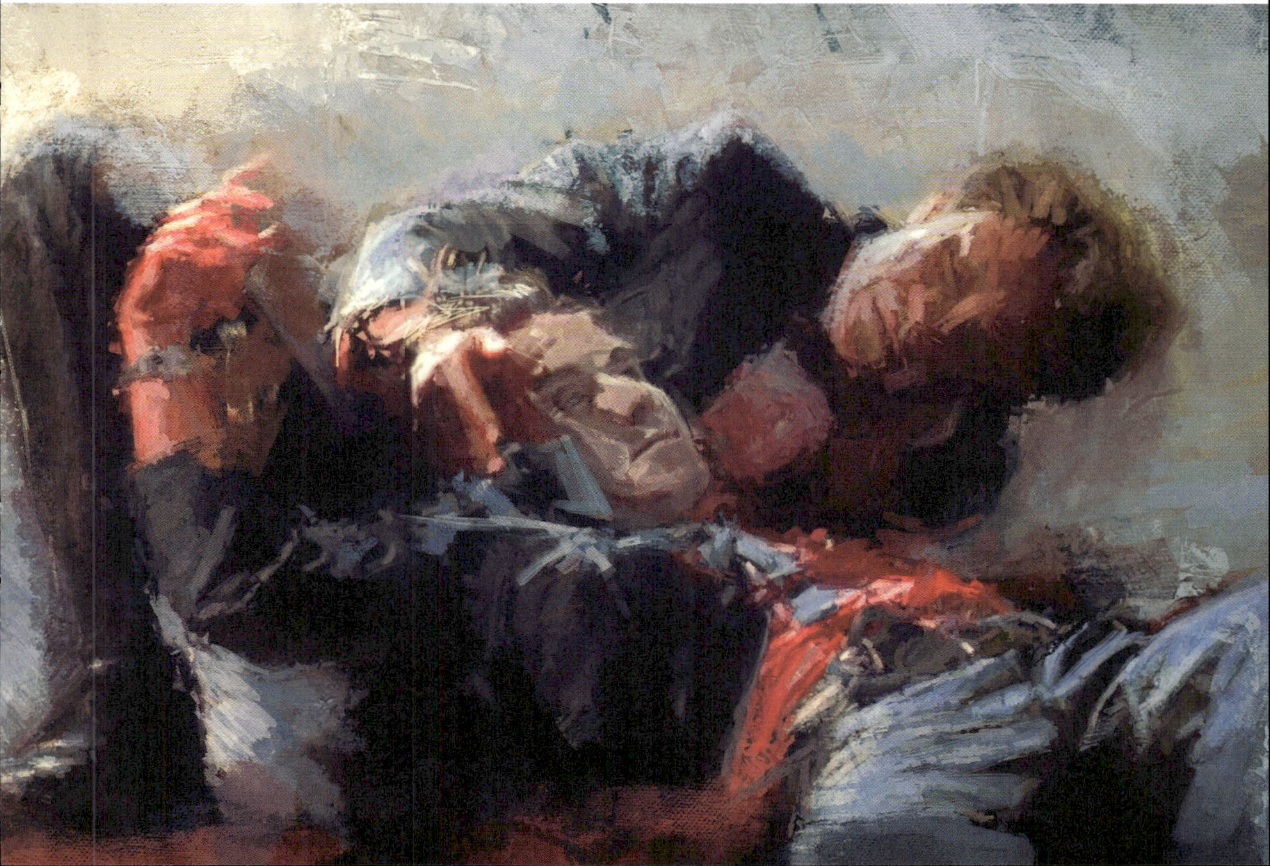

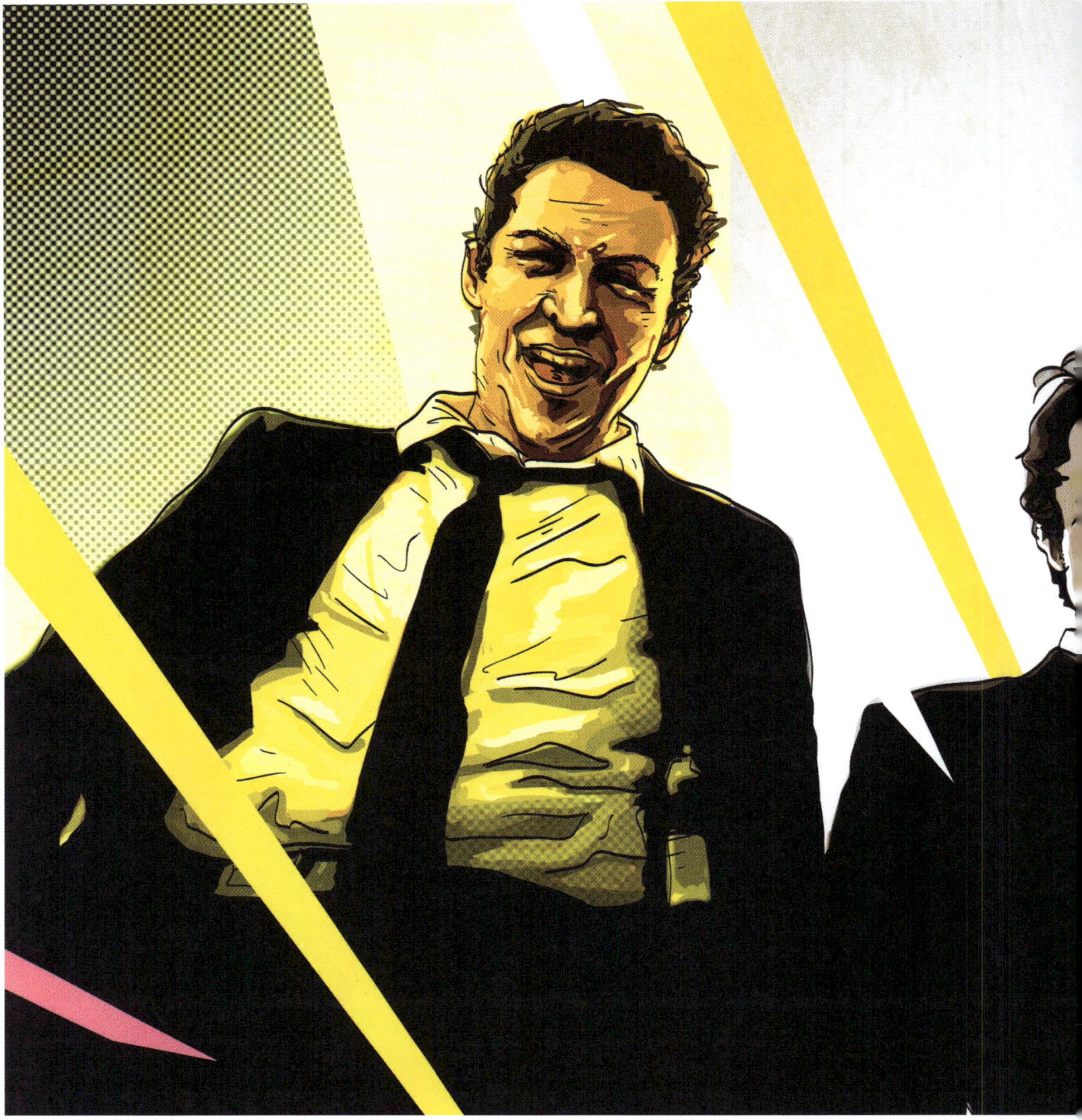

LOW-ANGLE SHOT

Contrapicado

In photography and filmmaking, a low-angle shot is an oblique shot taken from below with the camera facing upwards. In audiovisual language, this serves to convey a situation of control, power, grandeur and self-confidence.

En fotografía y cine, el plano contrapicado es una angulación oblicua inferior de la cámara, la cual se coloca mirando hacia arriba. En el lenguaje audiovisual, esto sirve para transmitir una situación de control, poder, grandeza y seguridad.

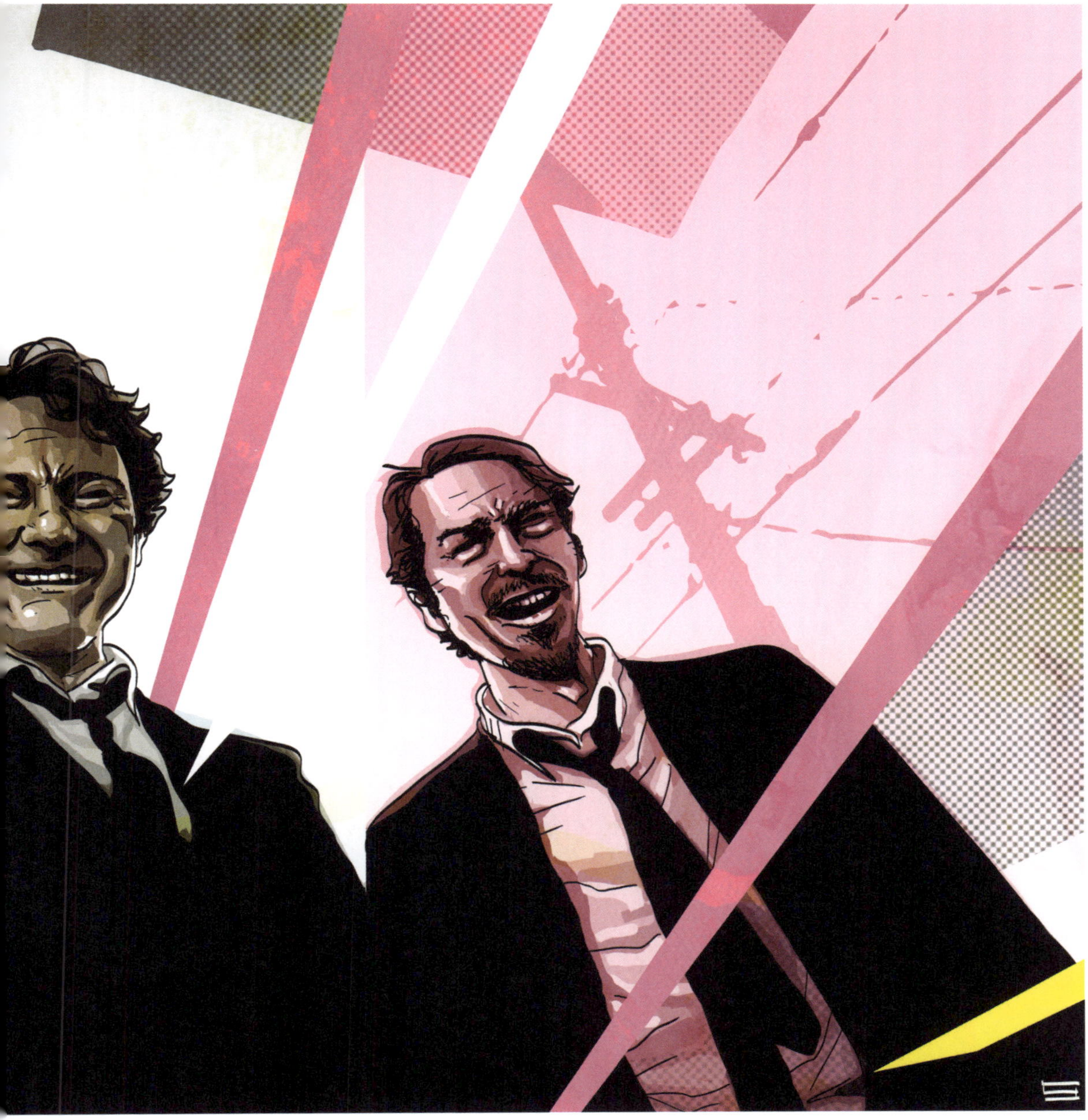

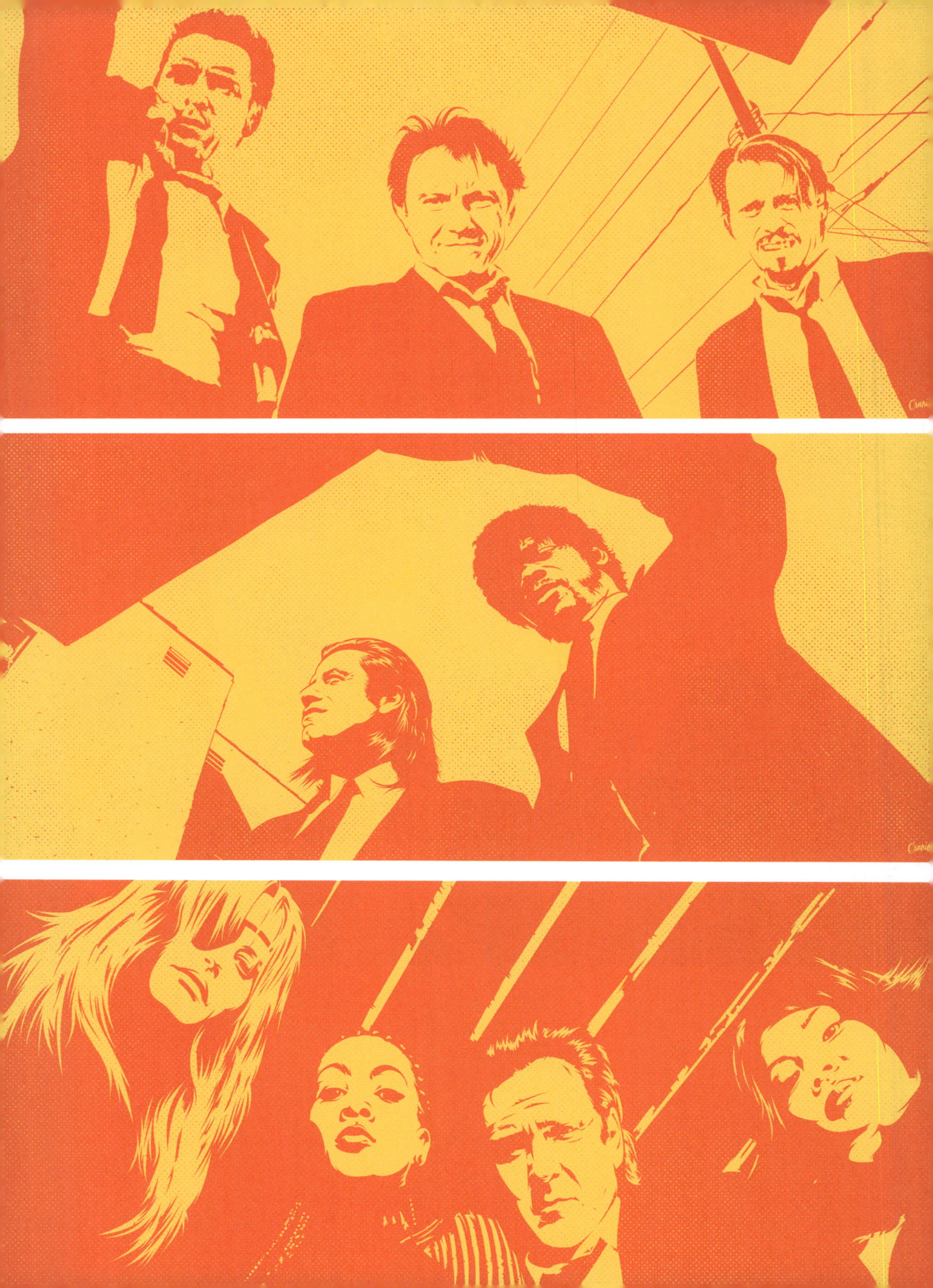

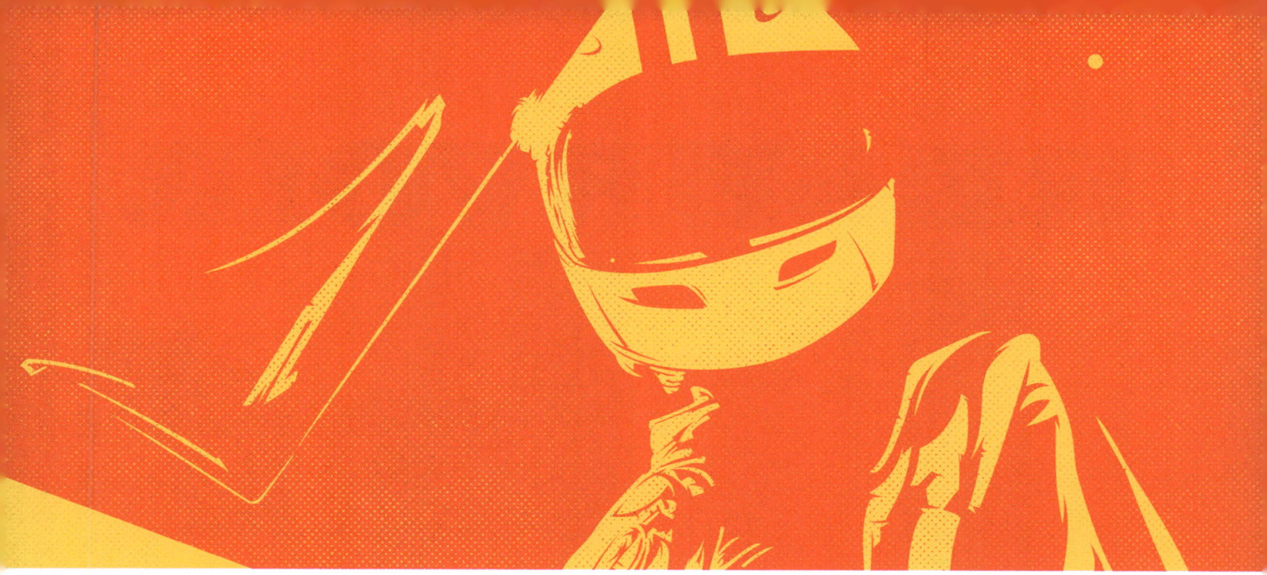

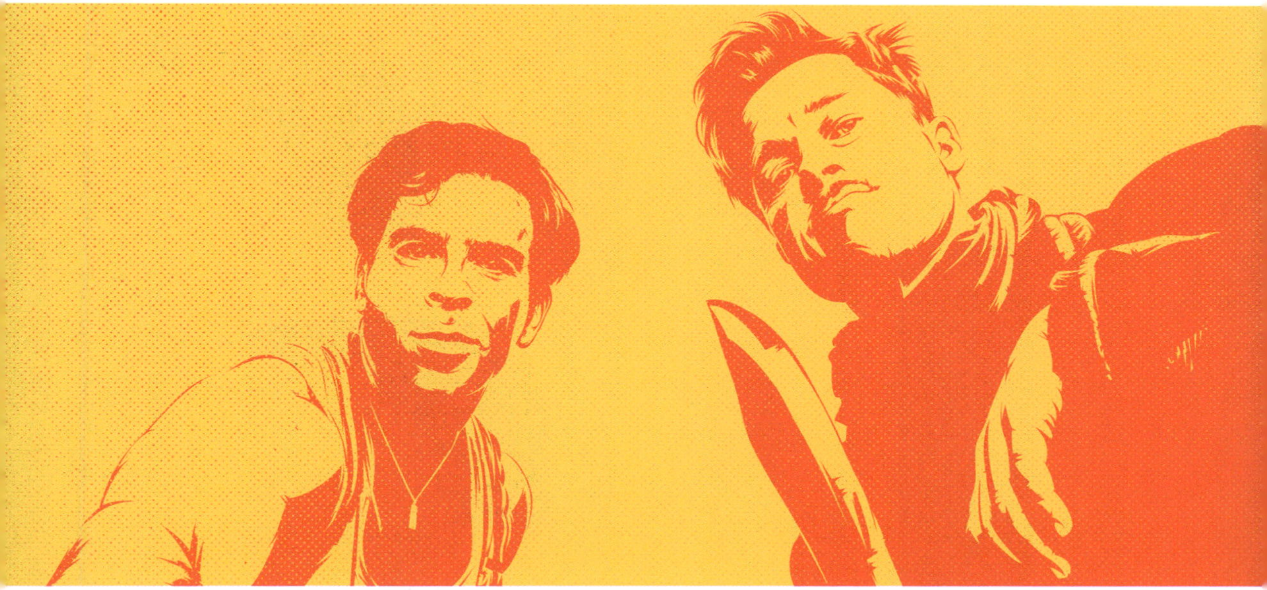

Low-angle shots are characteristic of Tarantino's cinema, usually with the camera placed in the open boot of a car. Tarantino did not invent this technique, but he has used it in most of his films.

Los planos contrapicados son característicos en el cine de Tarantino. Generalmente con la cámara colocada en el interior del maletero abierto de un coche. Tarantino no ha inventado esta técnica, pero sí que la ha utilizado en la mayoría de sus películas.

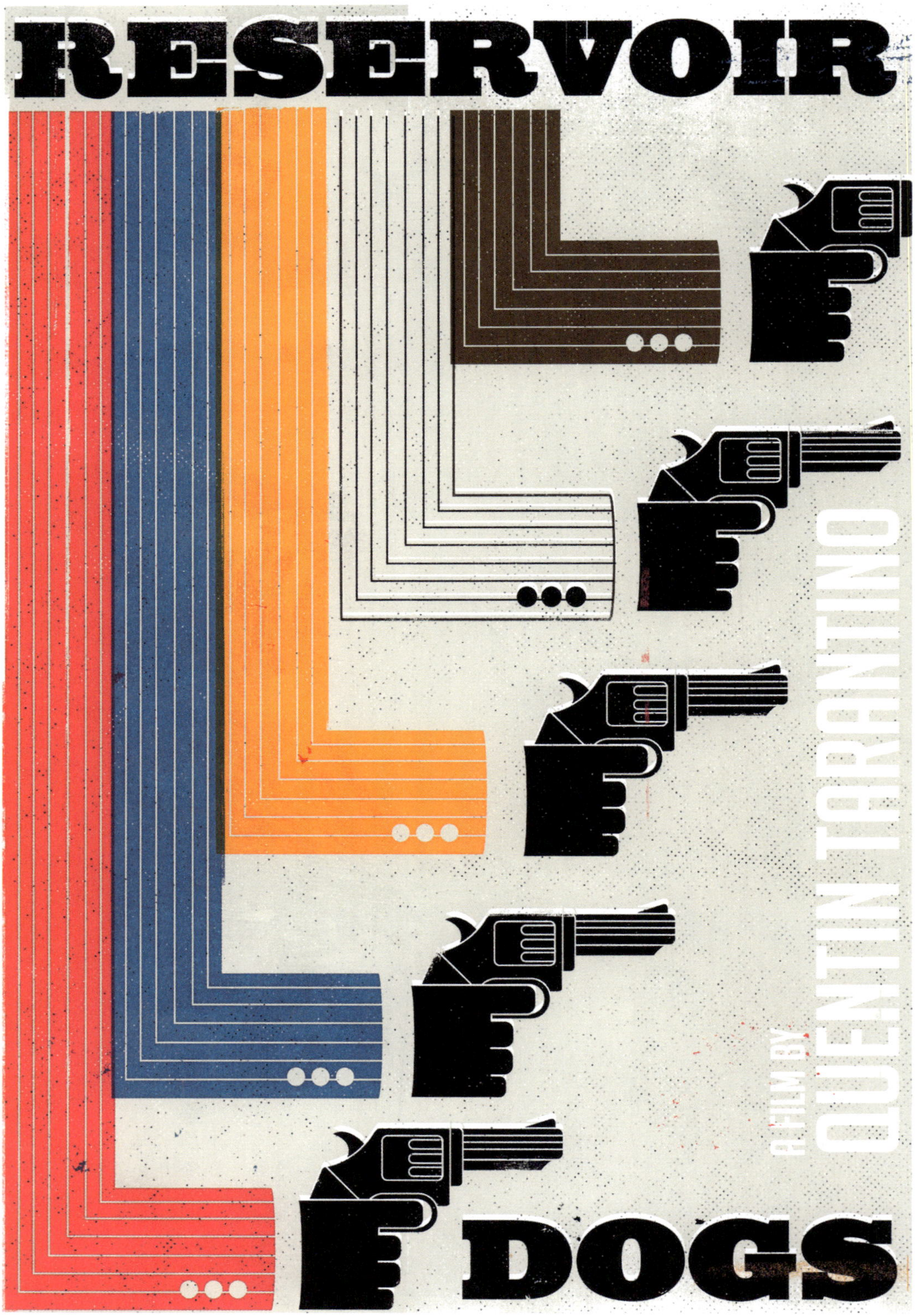
RESERVOIR
DOGS
A FILM BY
QUENTIN TARANTINO

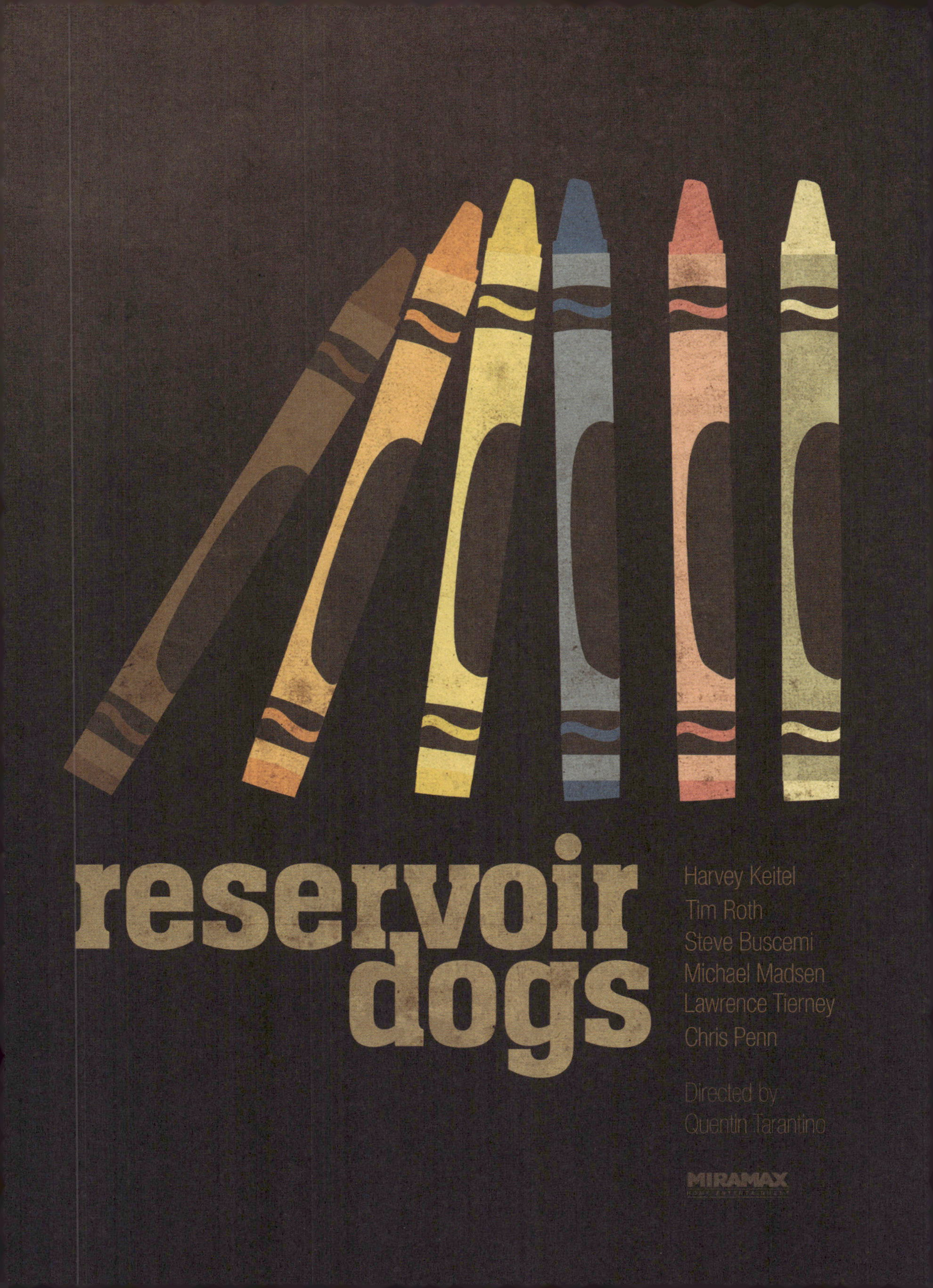
reservoir dogs
Harvey Keitel
Tim Roth
Steve Buscemi
Michael Madsen
Lawrence Tierney
Chris Penn
Directed by
Quentin Tarantino
MIRAMAX

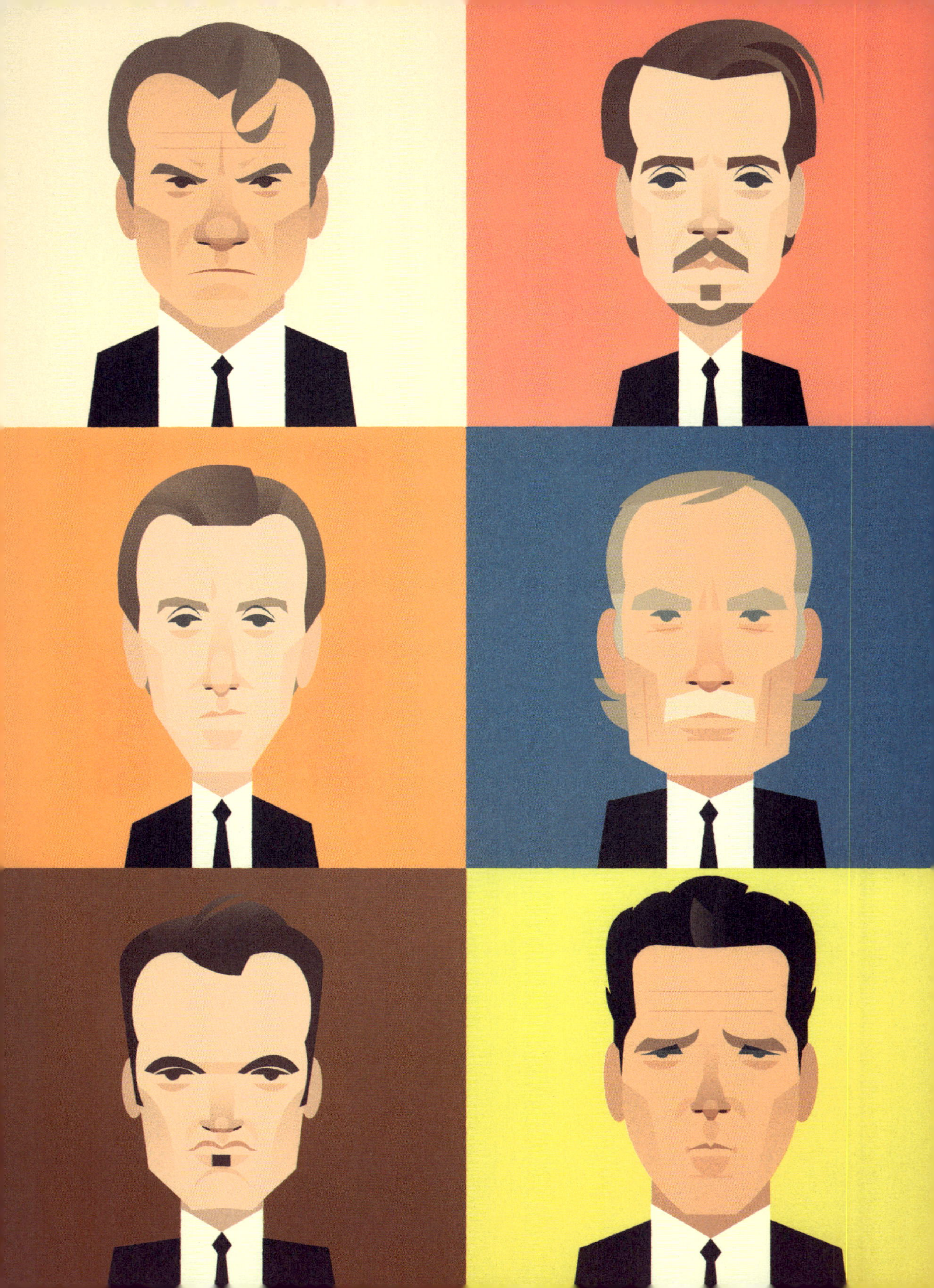

"The famous ear..."

"La famosa oreja..."

In the first screenings of the film, experts and some friends suggested that he delete the scene in which Mr. Blonde cuts off Marvin the policeman's ear while dancing to Stealers Wheel's "Stuck In The Middle With You". But the young 28-year-old director said, "This film is not meant to be for everyone, I made it for myself and everyone else is invited".

For the sake of amusement, Quentin Tarantino would count how many people left the cinema when the ear scene came. "The highest number to leave in a single session was 33," recalls the director.

En las primeras proyecciones de la película, los expertos y algunos amigos le sugirieron que eliminase la escena en la que el Sr. Rubio le corta la oreja al policía Marvin, mientras baila al son de "Stuck In The Middle With You" de Stealers Wheel. Pero este joven director de 28 expresó "esta película no pretende ser para todo el mundo, la hice para mí mismo y todos los demás están invitados".

Quentin Tarantino hizo el divertido ejercicio de contar cuántas personas abandonaban la sala cuando llegaba la escena de la oreja. "La cifra más alta de abandonos en una sola sesión fue de 33", recuerda el director.

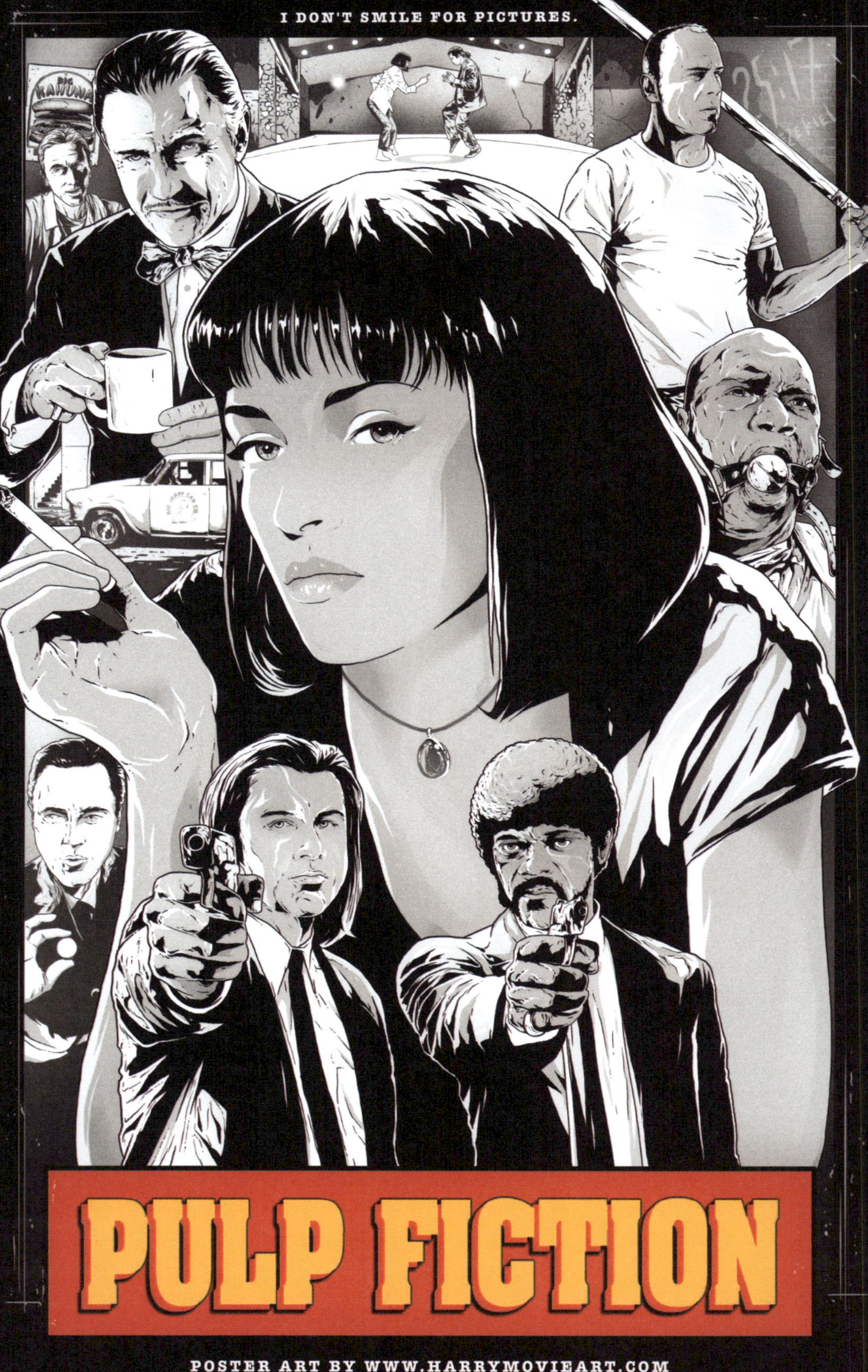
I DON'T SMILE FOR PICTURES.
PULP FICTION
POSTER ART BY WWW.HARRYMOVIEART.COM

PULP FICTION

1994

Although Reservoir Dogs endorsed filmmaker Quentin Tarantino's talent, there were several producers who refused to give the green light to Pulp Fiction because it was "too weird and too violent". One wonders how the executives concerned reacted after the film's release. In Pulp Fiction there are 3 actors who appeared in Reservoir Dogs: Harvey Keitel is "Mr. Wolf", Tim Roth is "Pumpkin", and Steve Buscemi is the waiter "Buddy Holly" at Jackrabbit Slim's restaurant.

It goes without saying that the recovery of a lost and forgotten John Travolta for the film industry is the work of Tarantino, taking a personal risk and giving him an unforgettable role. But in general, the film has a truly inspired, outstanding cast; from a memorable Bruce Willis to a fascinating Uma Thurman, and a loquacious evangelical and ruthless Samuel L. Jackson.

Aunque Reservoir Dogs avalaba al cineasta Quentin Tarantino, hubo diferentes productoras que se negaban a dar luz verde a Pulp Fiction por "demasiado rara y demasiado violenta". Cabe preguntarse qué caras pusieron los ejecutivos de turno tras el estreno del filme.
En Pulp Fiction encontramos a 3 actores que repiten después de Reservoir Dogs: Harvey Keitel es el "Señor Lobo", Tim Roth es "Pumpkin", y Steve Buscemi el camarero "Buddy Holly" en el restaurante Jackrabbit Slim's.

Ni que decir tiene que la recuperación de un denostado y olvidado John Travolta para el cine, es obra de Tarantino. De su apuesta personal y de darle un personaje inolvidable. Pero en general, la película posee un reparto coral muy inspirado, sobresaliente. Desde un Bruce Willis memorable a una fascinante Uma Thurman, o a un locuaz evangélico y despiadado Samuel L. Jackson.

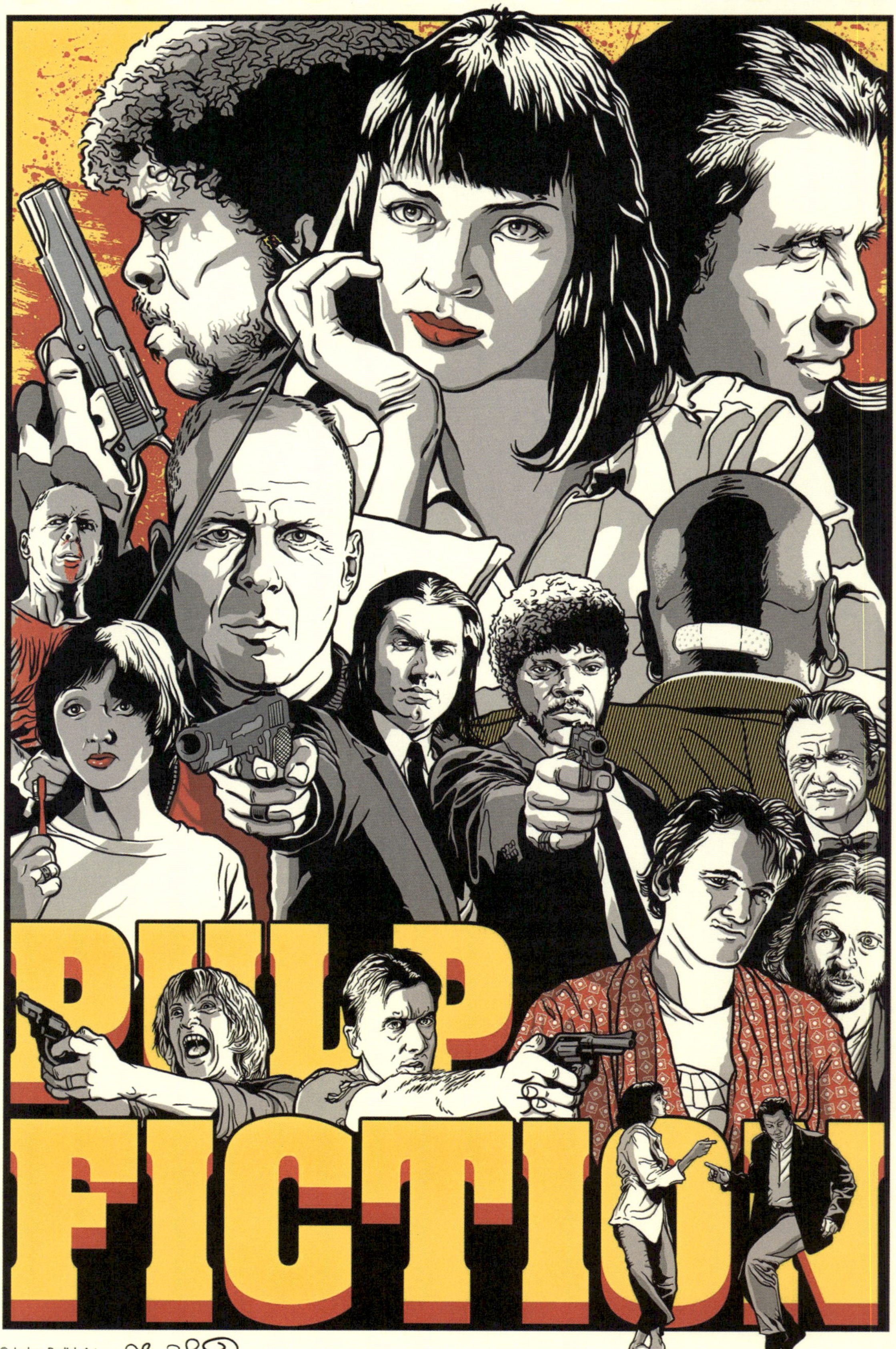
PULP
FICTION

"Everybody be cool this is a robbery! Any of you fuckin' pricks move and I'll execute every motherfucking last one of you"

"¡Todo el mundo quieto! ¡Esto es un atraco! ¡Y como algún jodido capullo se mueva, me cago en la leche, me pienso cargar hasta el último de vosotros!"

- Pumpkin & Honey Bunny -

pulp fiction.

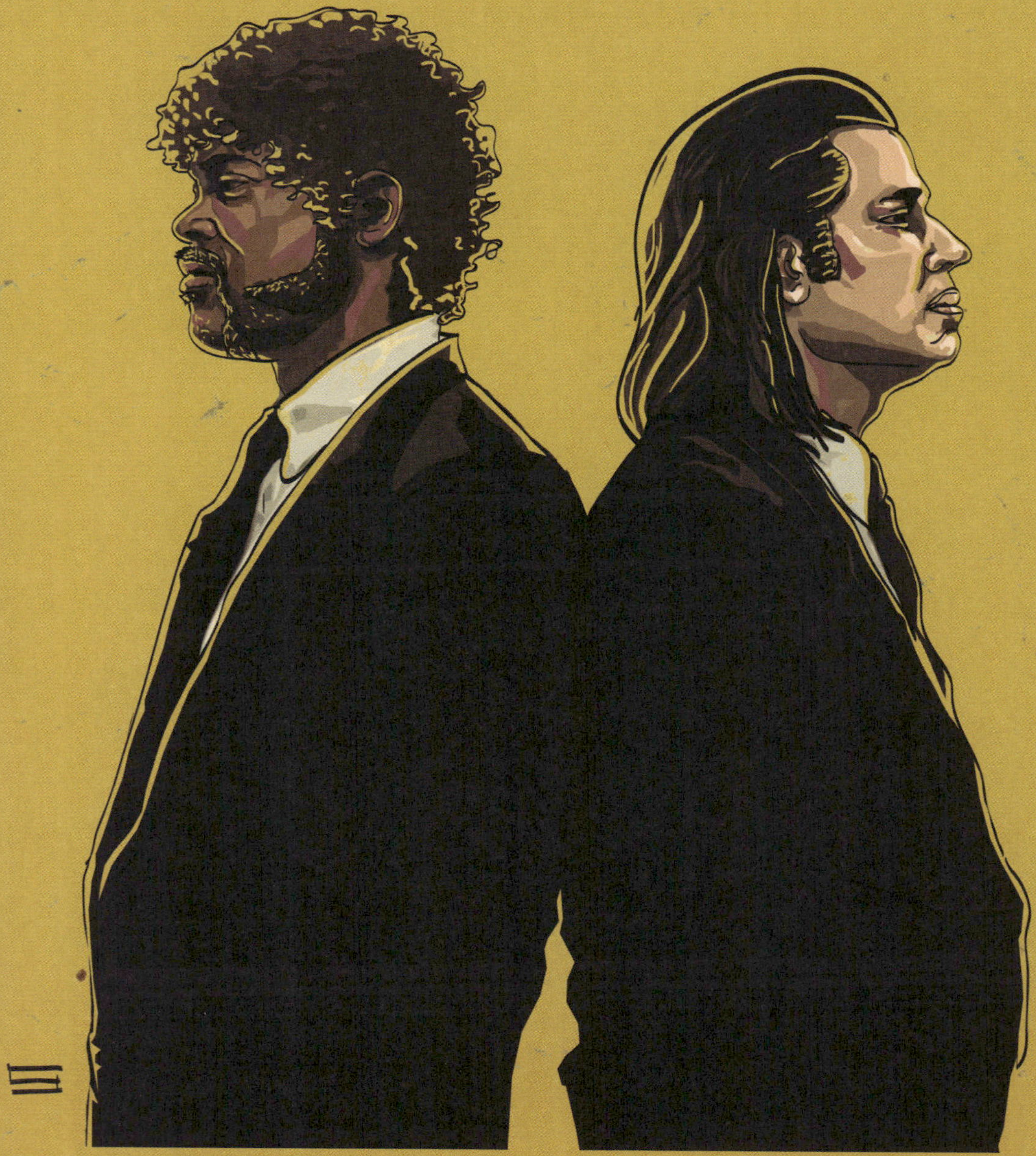

Jules Winnfield

Jules is a hitman who works for Marsellus Wallace. He has a certain spiritual nature, and after escaping unharmed from a gunfight with Vincent Vega, he considers it a miracle and decides to quit criminal life.

Es un asesino a sueldo que trabaja para Marsellus Wallace. Tiene un cierto carácter espiritual, y tras salir ileso de un tiroteo junto a Vincent Vega, lo considera un milagro, por lo que decide dejar la vida criminal.

Vicent Vega

Vega is one of the main characters of "Pulp Fiction" and appears in all three of the film's stories. He is a long haired hitman and regular drug user. As he himself says, he can't stand orders or requests unless they are made politely.
Curiosity: In the Tarantino universe, Vincent Vega is the brother of Vic Vega, the psychopathic criminal played by the actor Michael Madsen in "Reservoir Dogs" Tarantino once expressed his intention to shoot a prequel to both films called "The Vega Brothers," but the project never materialised.

Es uno de los personajes principales de "Pulp Fiction" y que atraviesa las tres historias de la película, un sicario de pelo largo y asiduo consumidor de drogas. Como él mismo afirma, no soporta las órdenes ni las peticiones si no hay cortesía de por medio.
Curiosidad: Vincent Vega, dentro del universo Tarantino, es hermano de Vic Vega, el delincuente psicópata que interpreta el actor Michael Madsen en "Reservoir Dogs". Tarantino alguna vez manifestó su intención de rodar una precuela a ambas películas llamada "The Vega Brothers", pero el proyecto nunca se materializó.

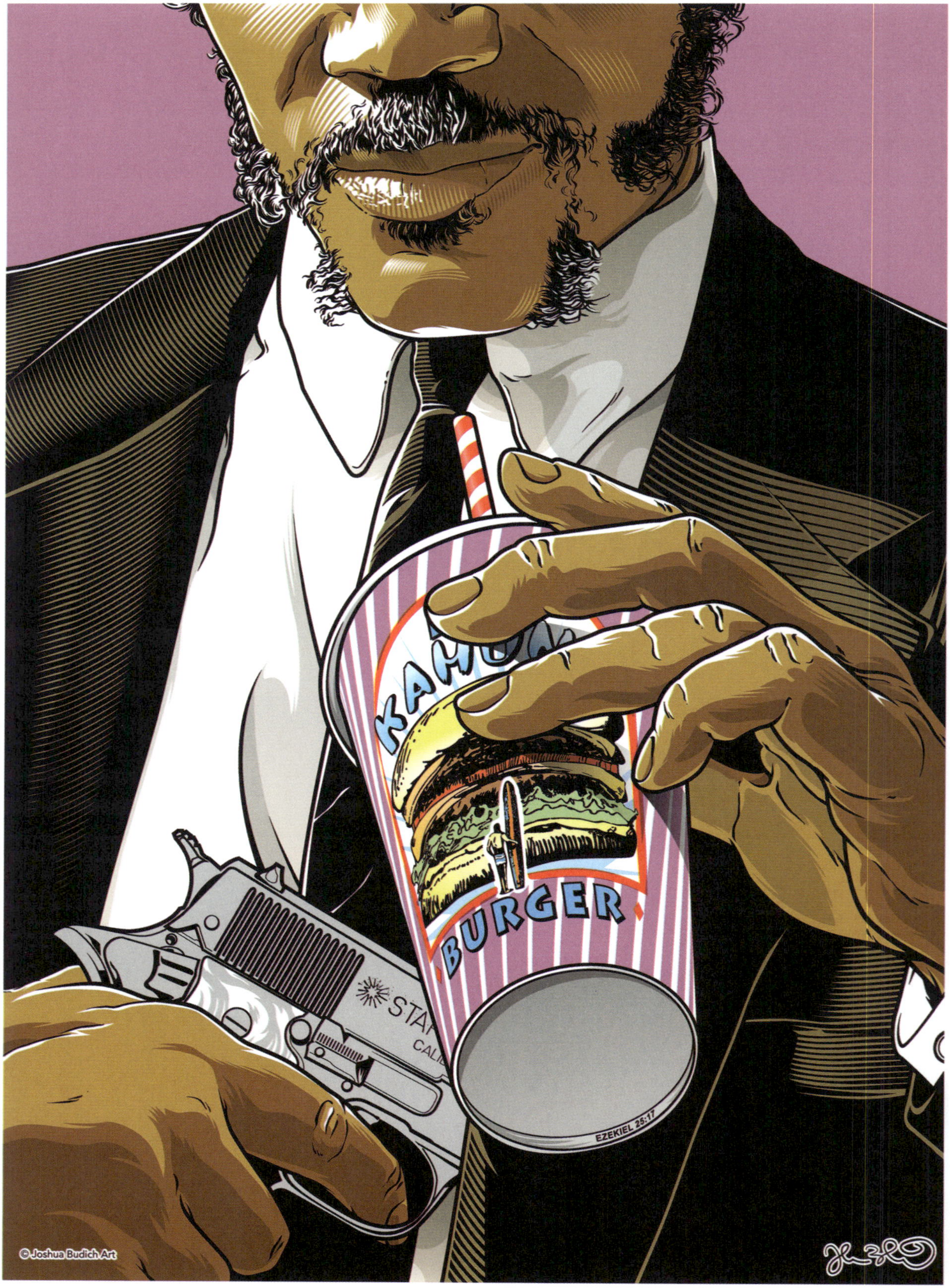
BURGER
EZEKIEL 25:17
© Joshua Budich Art

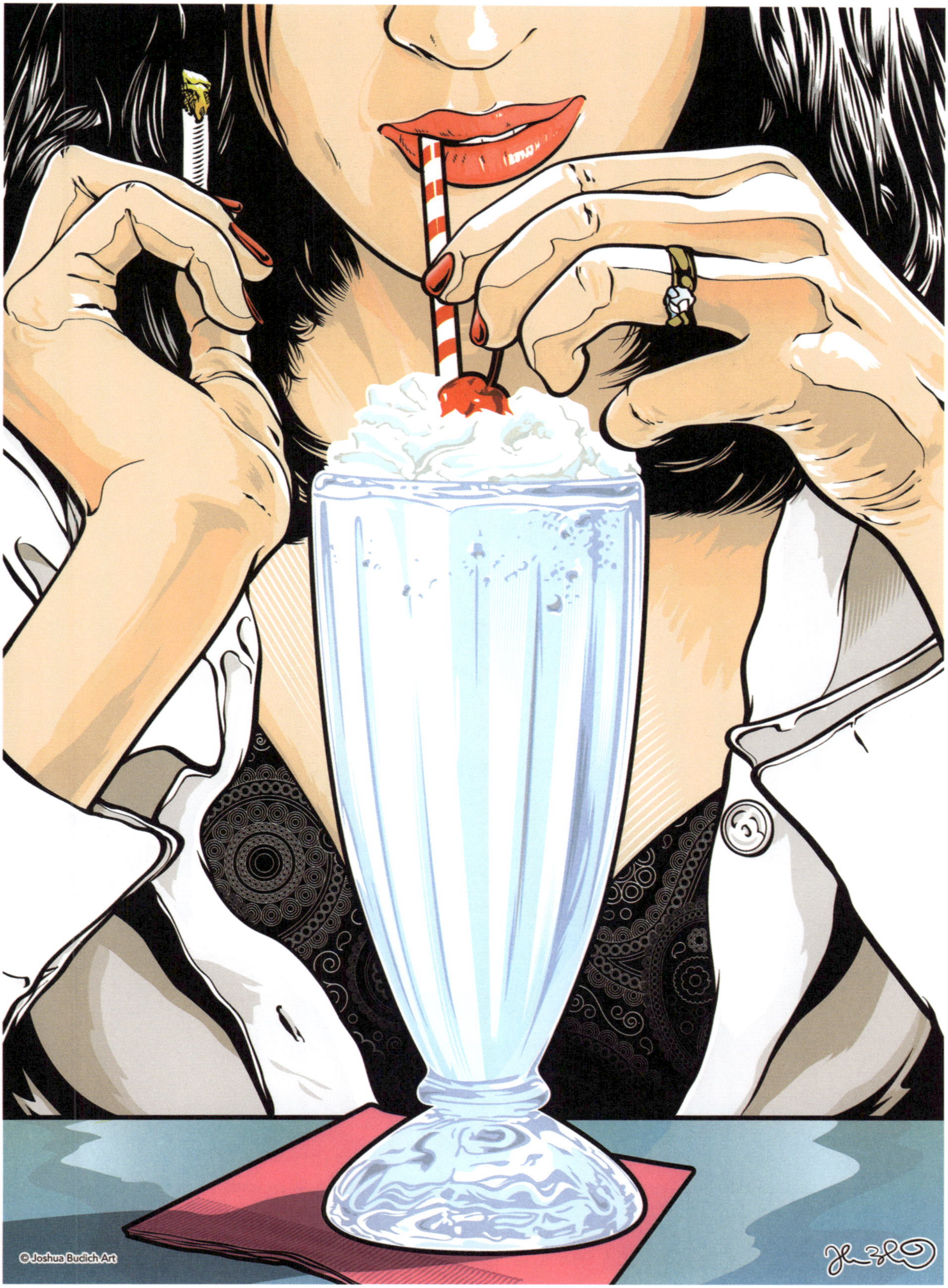
© Joshua Budich Art

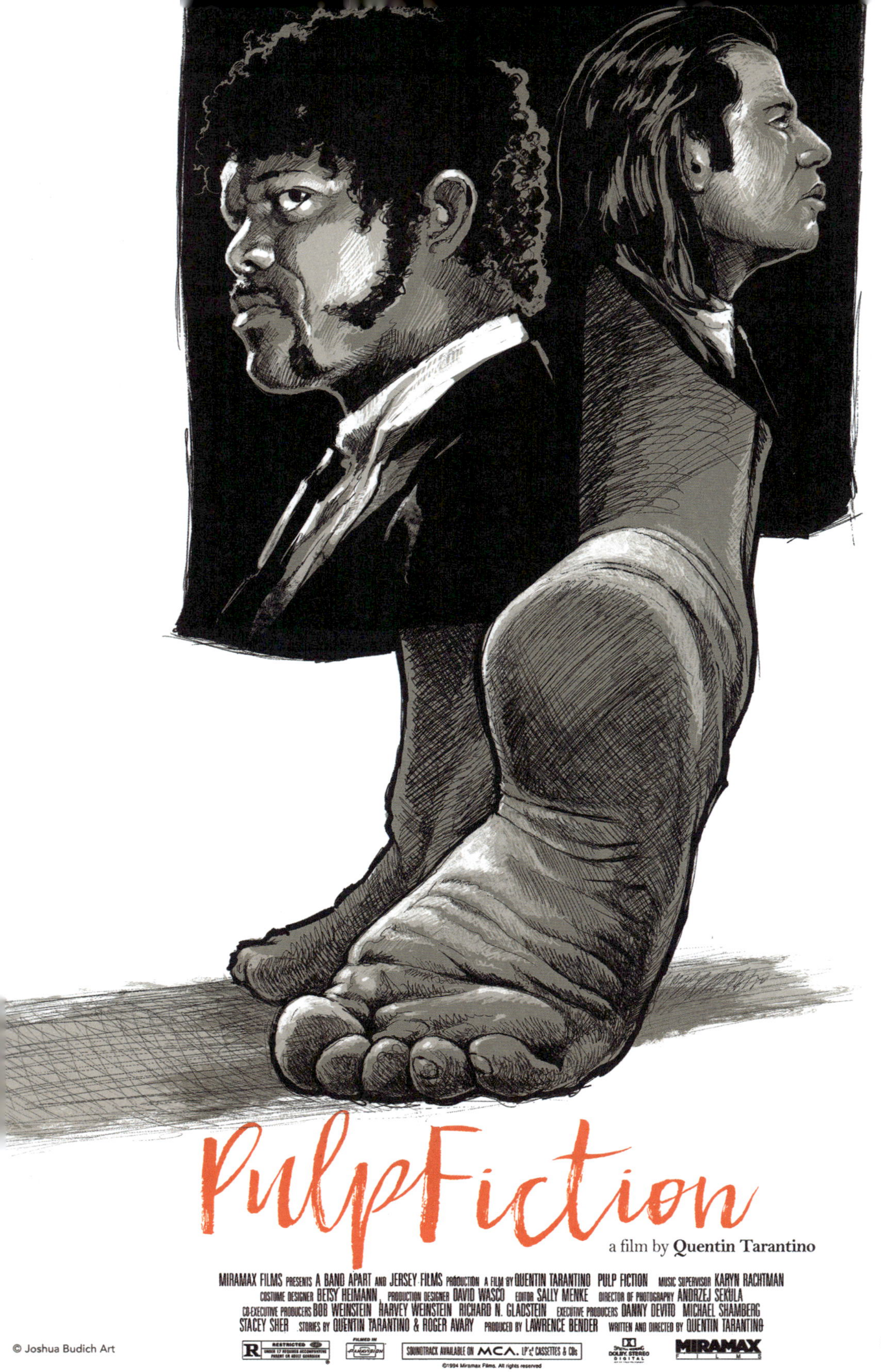

PulpFiction
a film by Quentin Tarantino
MIRAMAX FILMS PRESENTS A BAND APART AND JERSEY FILMS PRODUCTION A FILM BY QUENTIN TARANTINO PULP FICTION MUSIC SUPERVISOR KARYN RACHTMAN
COSTUME DESIGNER BETSY HEIMANN PRODUCTION DESIGNER DAVID WASCO EDITOR SALLY MENKE DIRECTOR OF PHOTOGRAPHY ANDRZEJ SEKULA
CO-EXECUTIVE PRODUCERS BOB WEINSTEIN HARVEY WEINSTEIN RICHARD N. GLADSTEIN EXECUTIVE PRODUCERS DANNY DEVITO MICHAEL SHAMBERG
STACEY SHER STORIES BY QUENTIN TARANTINO & ROGER AVARY PRODUCED BY LAWRENCE BENDER WRITTEN AND DIRECTED BY QUENTIN TARANTINO
R RESTRICTED
FILMED IN PANAVISION
SOUNDTRACK AVAILABLE ON MCA. LP's CASSETTES & CDs
DOLBY STEREO DIGITAL
MIRAMAX FILMS
©1994 Miramax Films. All rights reserved

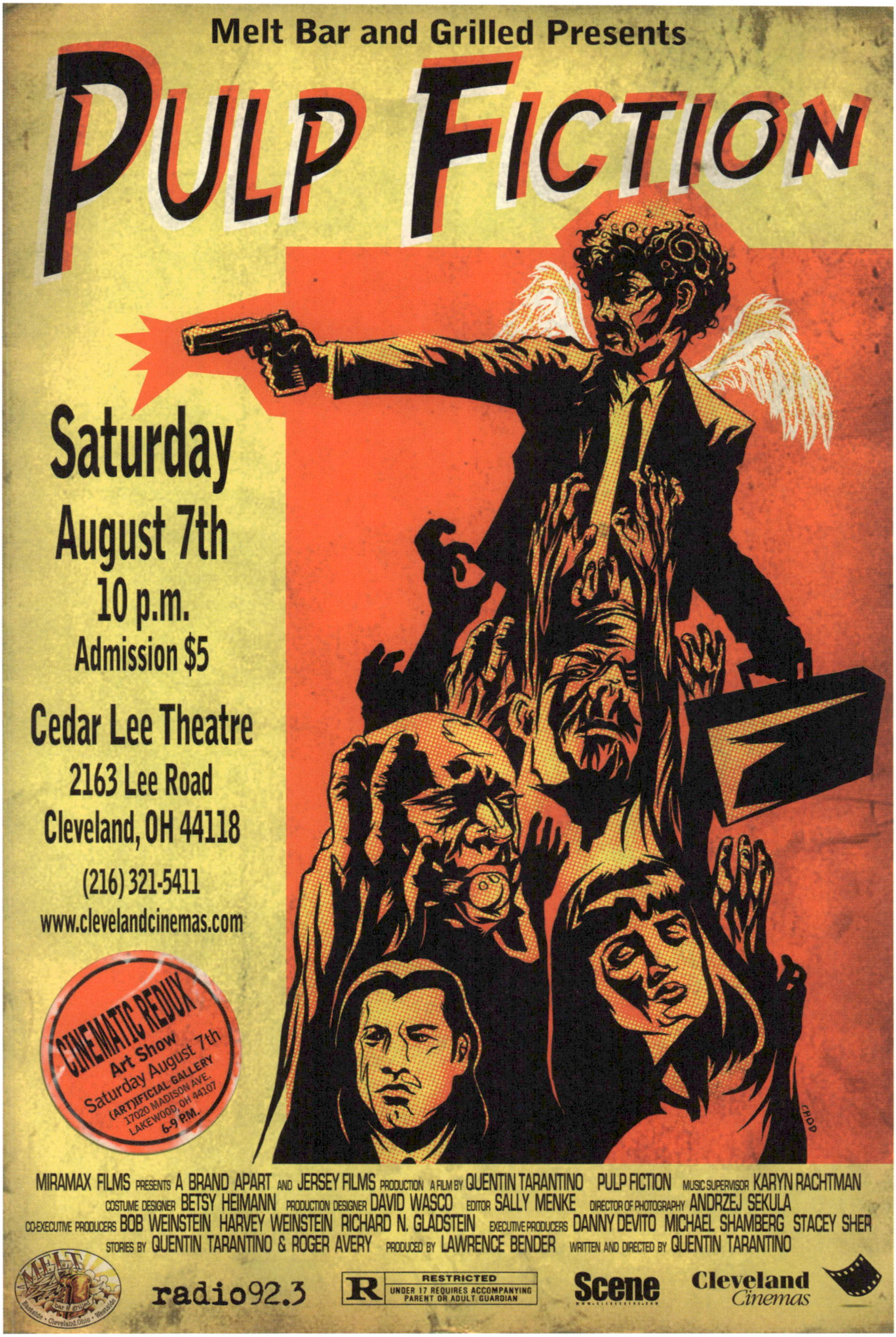
Melt Bar and Grilled Presents
PULP FICTION
Saturday
August 7th
10 p.m.
Admission $5
Cedar Lee Theatre
2163 Lee Road
Cleveland, OH 44118
(216) 321-5411
www.clevelandcinemas.com
CINEMATIC REDUX
Art Show
Saturday August 7th
(ART)IFICIAL GALLERY
17020 MADISON AVE.
LAKEWOOD, OH 44107
6-9 P.M.
CHOD
MIRAMAX FILMS PRESENTS A BRAND APART AND JERSEY FILMS PRODUCTION A FILM BY QUENTIN TARANTINO PULP FICTION MUSIC SUPERVISOR KARYN RACHTMAN
COSTUME DESIGNER BETSY HEIMANN PRODUCTION DESIGNER DAVID WASCO EDITOR SALLY MENKE DIRECTOR OF PHOTOGRAPHY ANDRZEJ SEKULA
CO-EXECUTIVE PRODUCERS BOB WEINSTEIN HARVEY WEINSTEIN RICHARD N. GLADSTEIN EXECUTIVE PRODUCERS DANNY DEVITO MICHAEL SHAMBERG STACEY SHER
STORIES BY QUENTIN TARANTINO & ROGER AVERY PRODUCED BY LAWRENCE BENDER WRITTEN AND DIRECTED BY QUENTIN TARANTINO
MELT bar & grilled Eastside • Cleveland, Ohio • Westside
radio92.3
R RESTRICTED UNDER 17 REQUIRES ACCOMPANYING PARENT OR ADULT GUARDIAN
Scene
Cleveland Cinemas

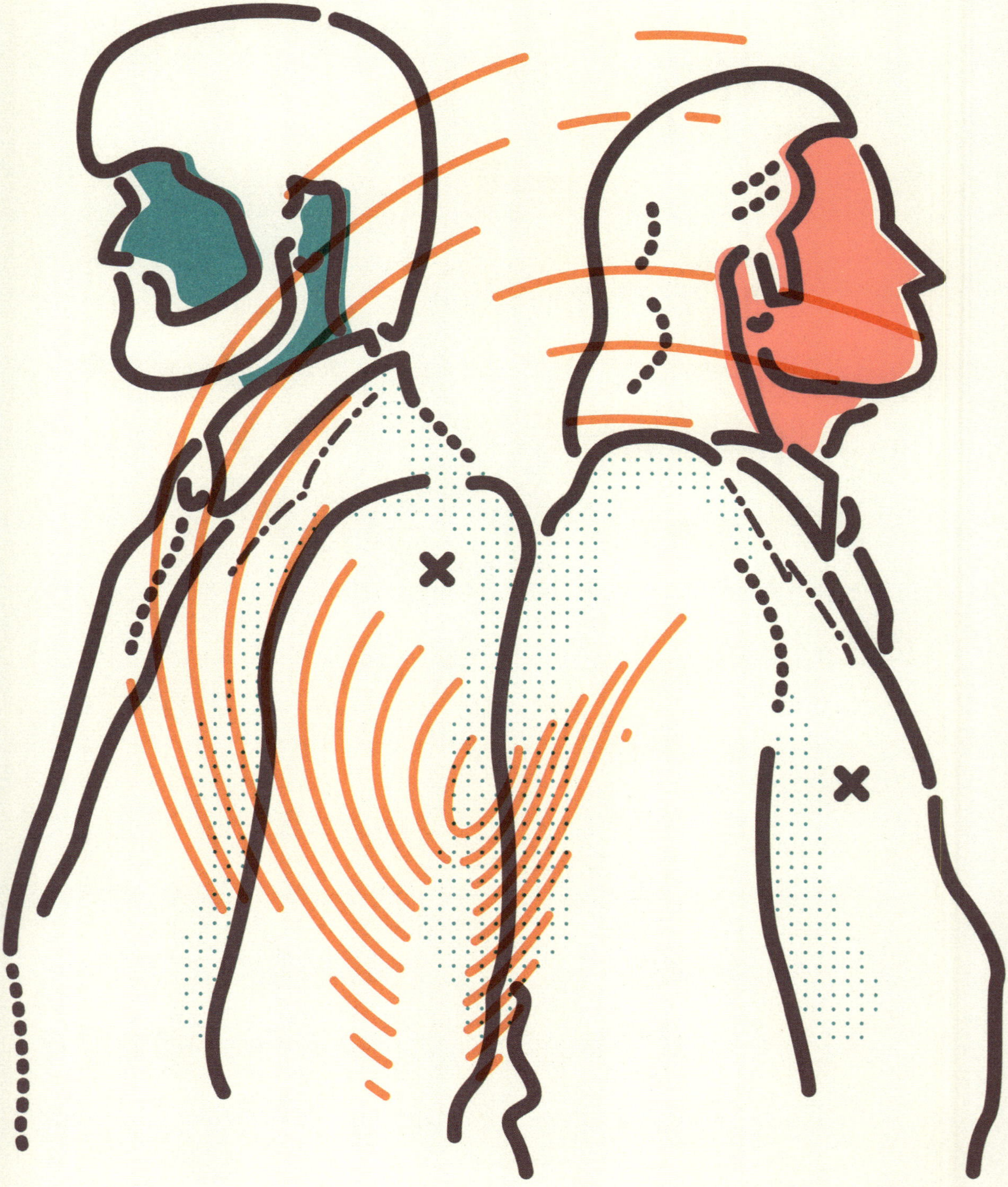

"You know what they call a Quarter Pounder with Cheese in Paris?"

"¿Sabes cómo llaman al cuarto de libra con queso en París?"

- Vicent Vega -

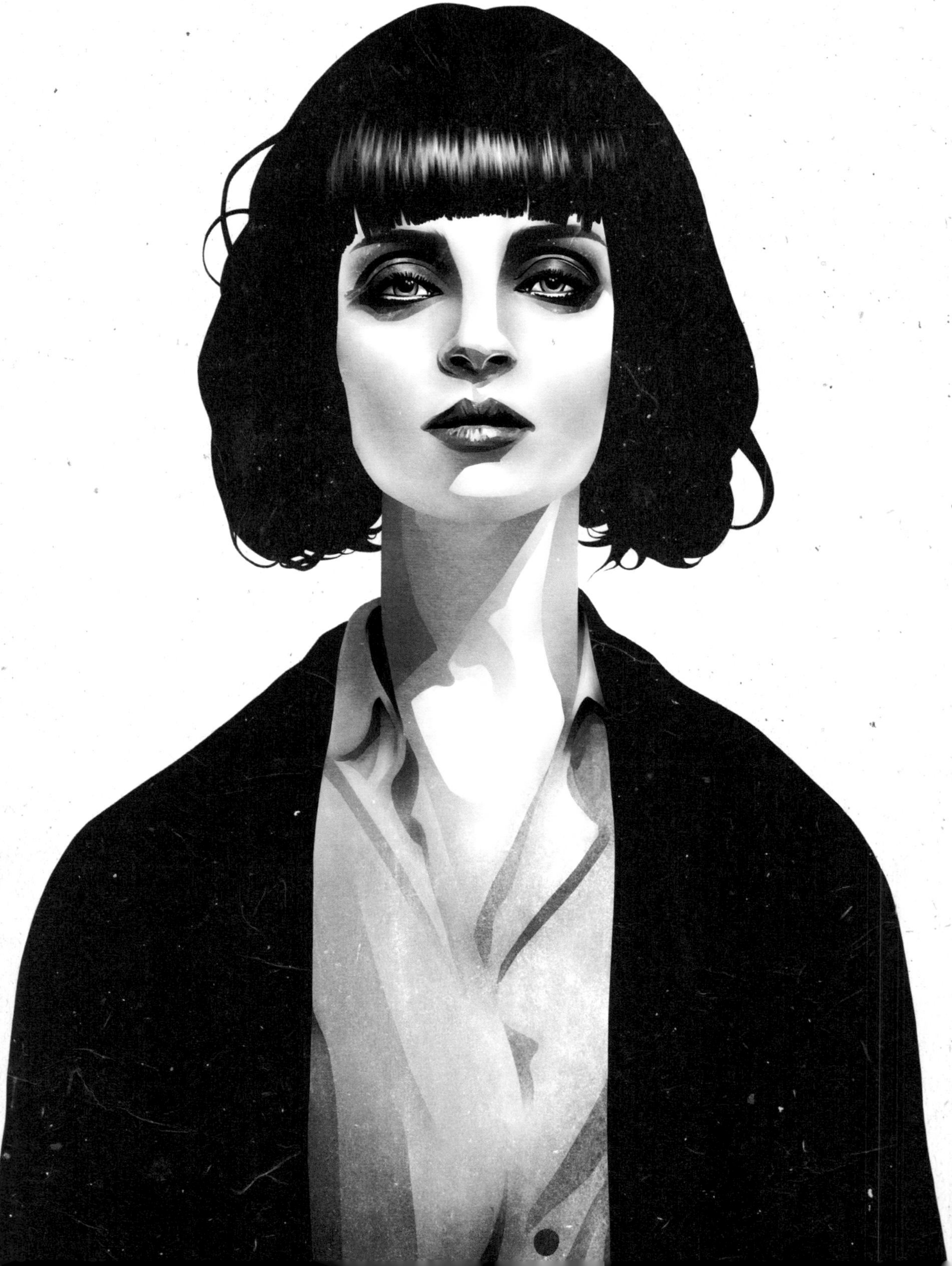

Girl, You'll Be a Woman Soon

Girl, you'll be a woman soon
I love you so much, can't count all the ways
I've died for you girl and all they can say is
"He's not your kind"
They never get tired of putting me down
And I'll never know when I come around
What I'm gonna find
Don't let them make up your mind
Don't you know, girl, you'll be a woman soon
Please, come take my hand
Girl, you'll be a woman soon
Soon, you'll need a man
I've been misunderstood for all of my life
But what they're saying girl it cuts like a knife
"The boy's no good"
Well, I've finally found what I'm a-looking for
But if they get their chance they'll end it for sure
Surely would
Baby, I've done all I could
Now it's up to you girl, you'll be a woman soon
Please, come take my hand
Girl, you'll be a woman soon
Soon, you'll need a man
Girl, you'll be a woman soon
Please, come take my hand
Girl, you'll be a woman soon
Soon but soon, you'll need a man
Girl, you'll be a woman soon
Please, come take my hand

Original song 1967 - Neil Diamond | Artist Urge Overkill | Album Pulp Fiction - 1994

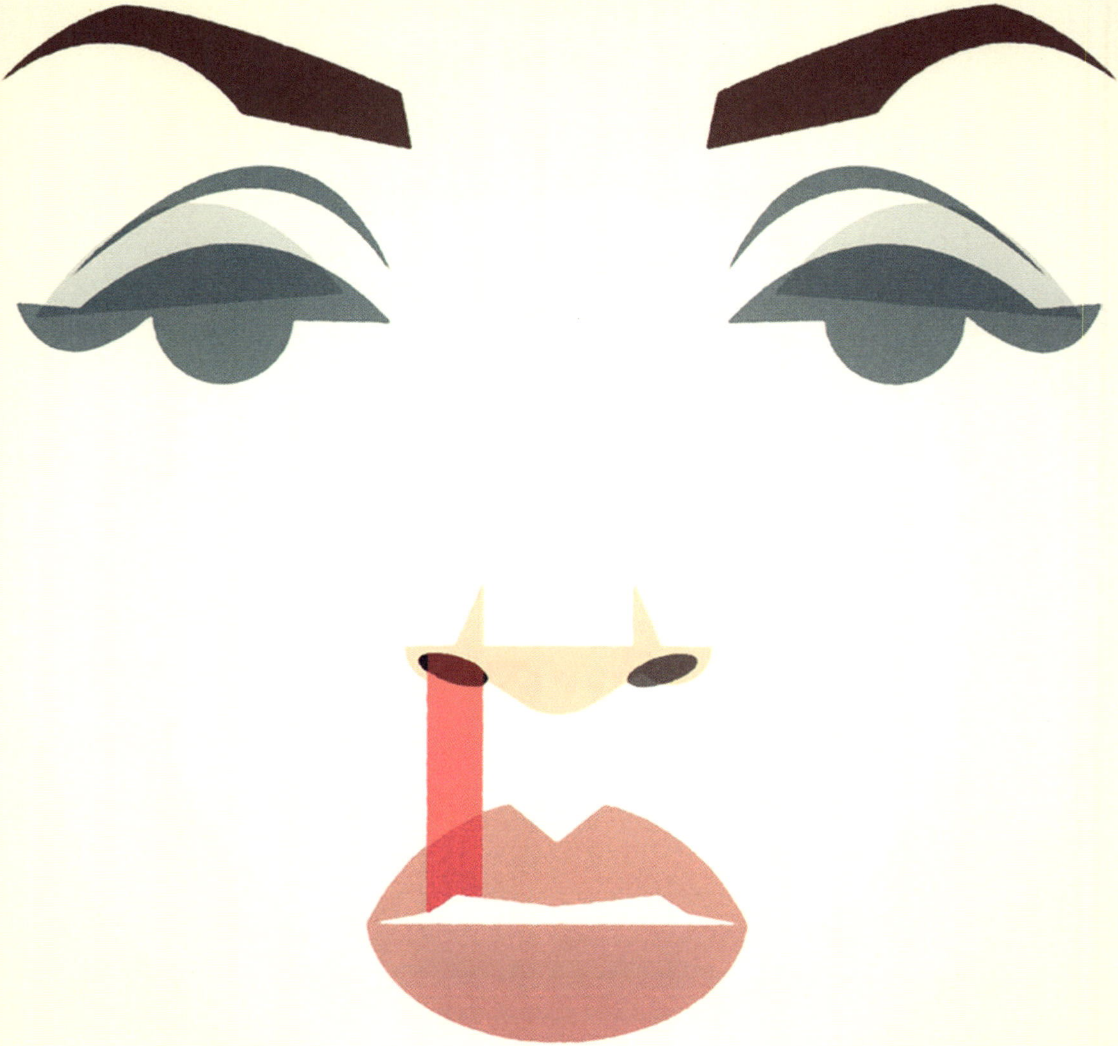

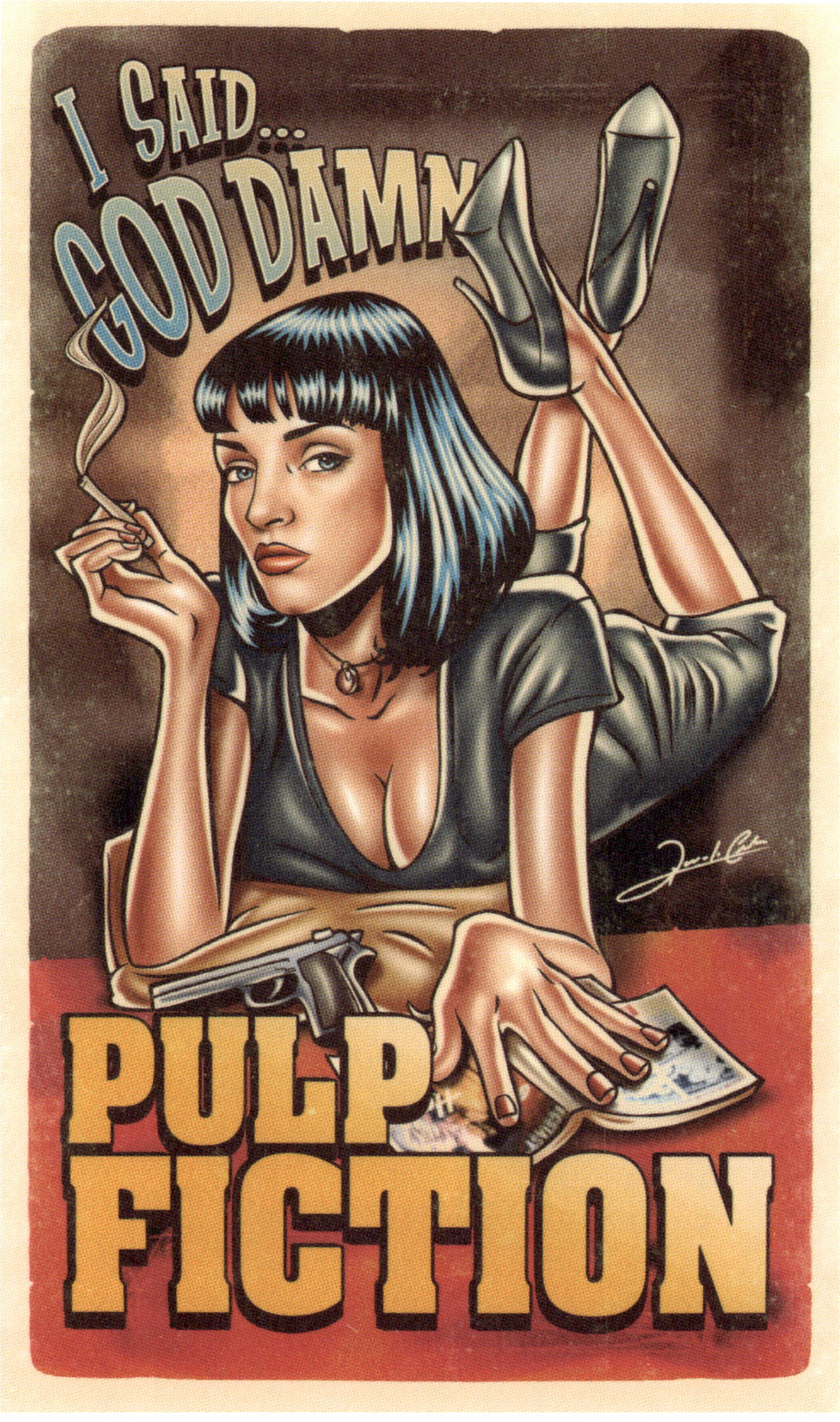
I SAID...
GOD DAMN
PULP
FICTION

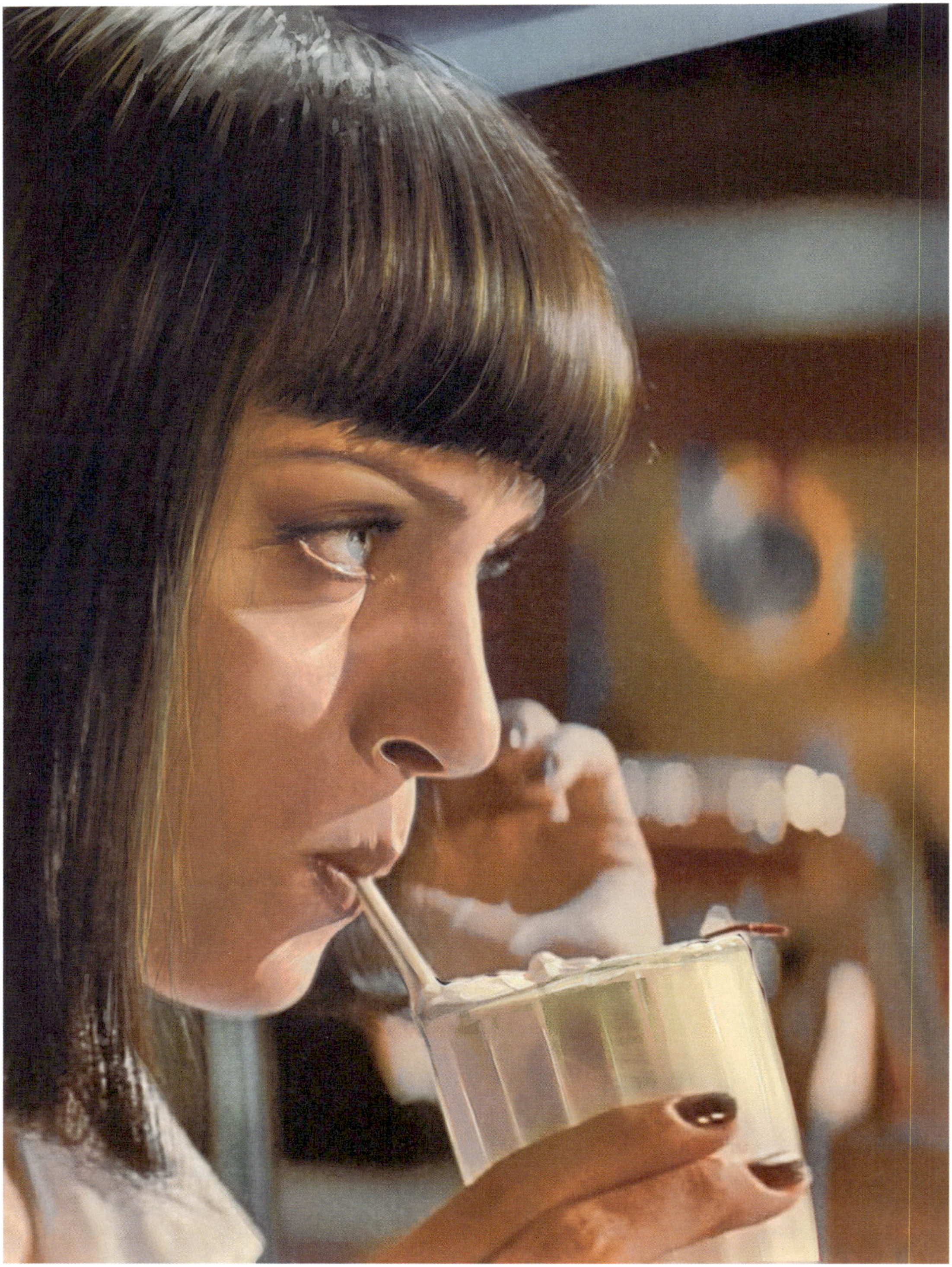

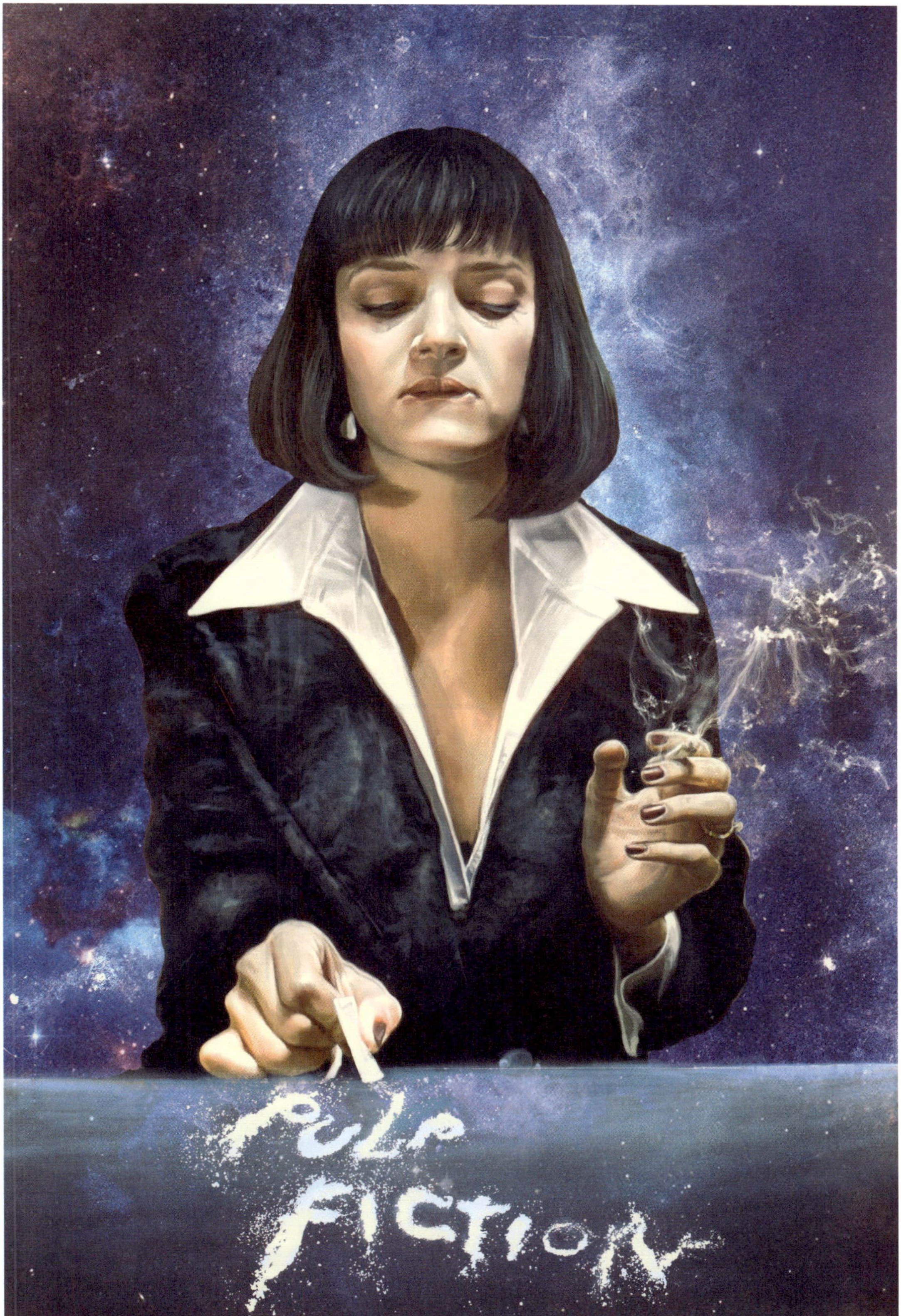
PULP
FICTION

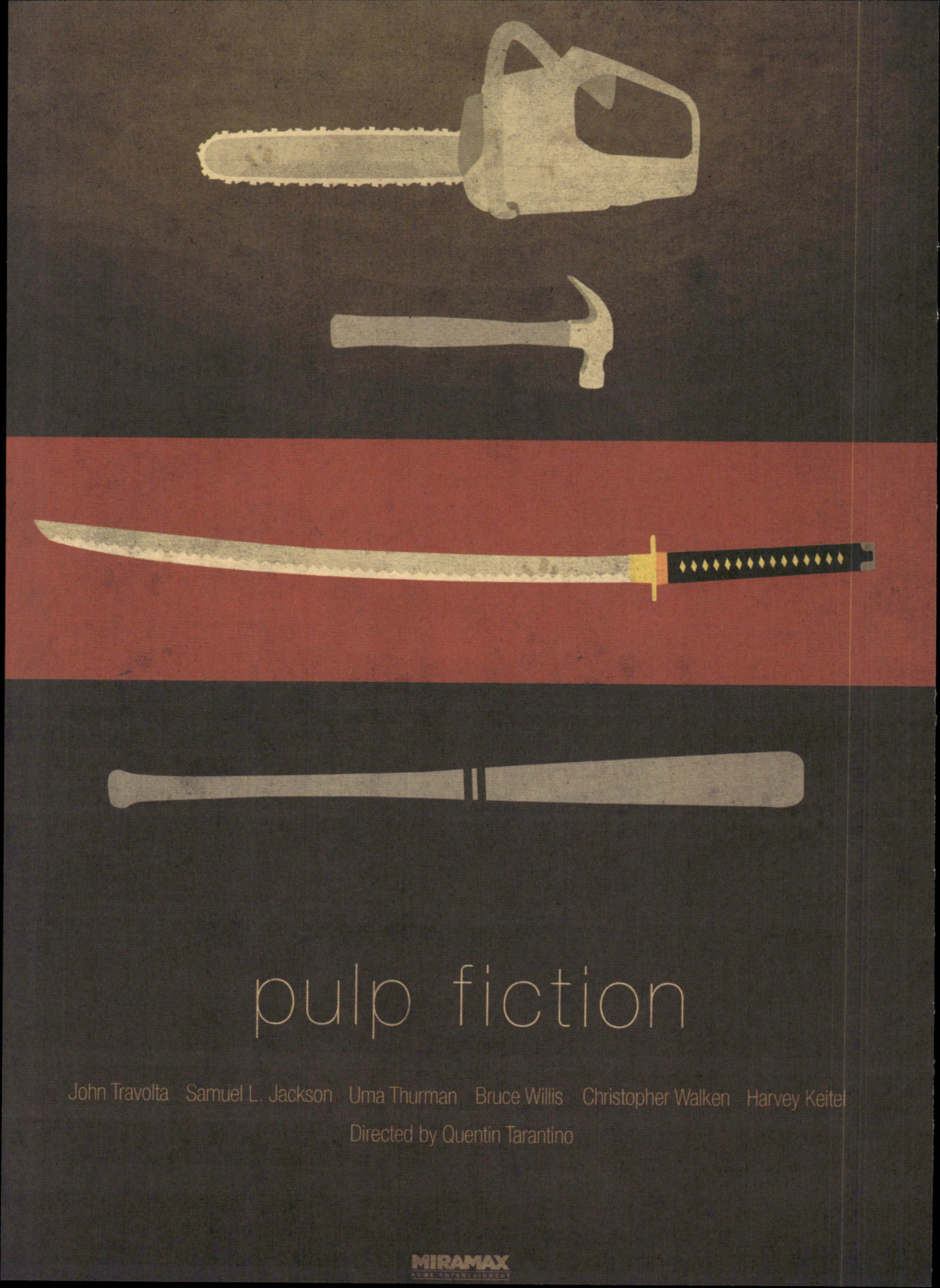
pulp fiction
John Travolta Samuel L. Jackson Uma Thurman Bruce Willis Christopher Walken Harvey Keitel
Directed by Quentin Tarantino
MIRAMAX

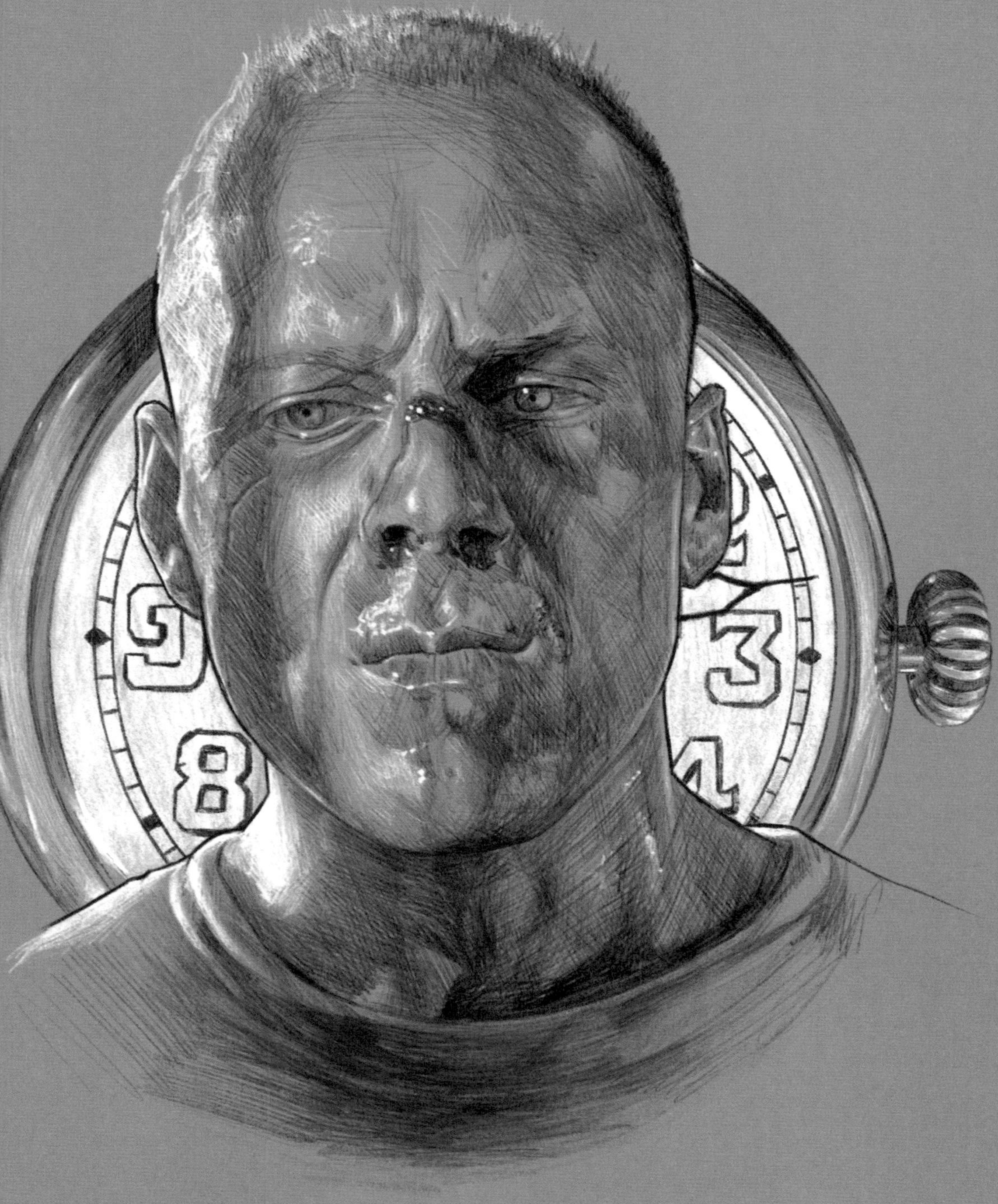

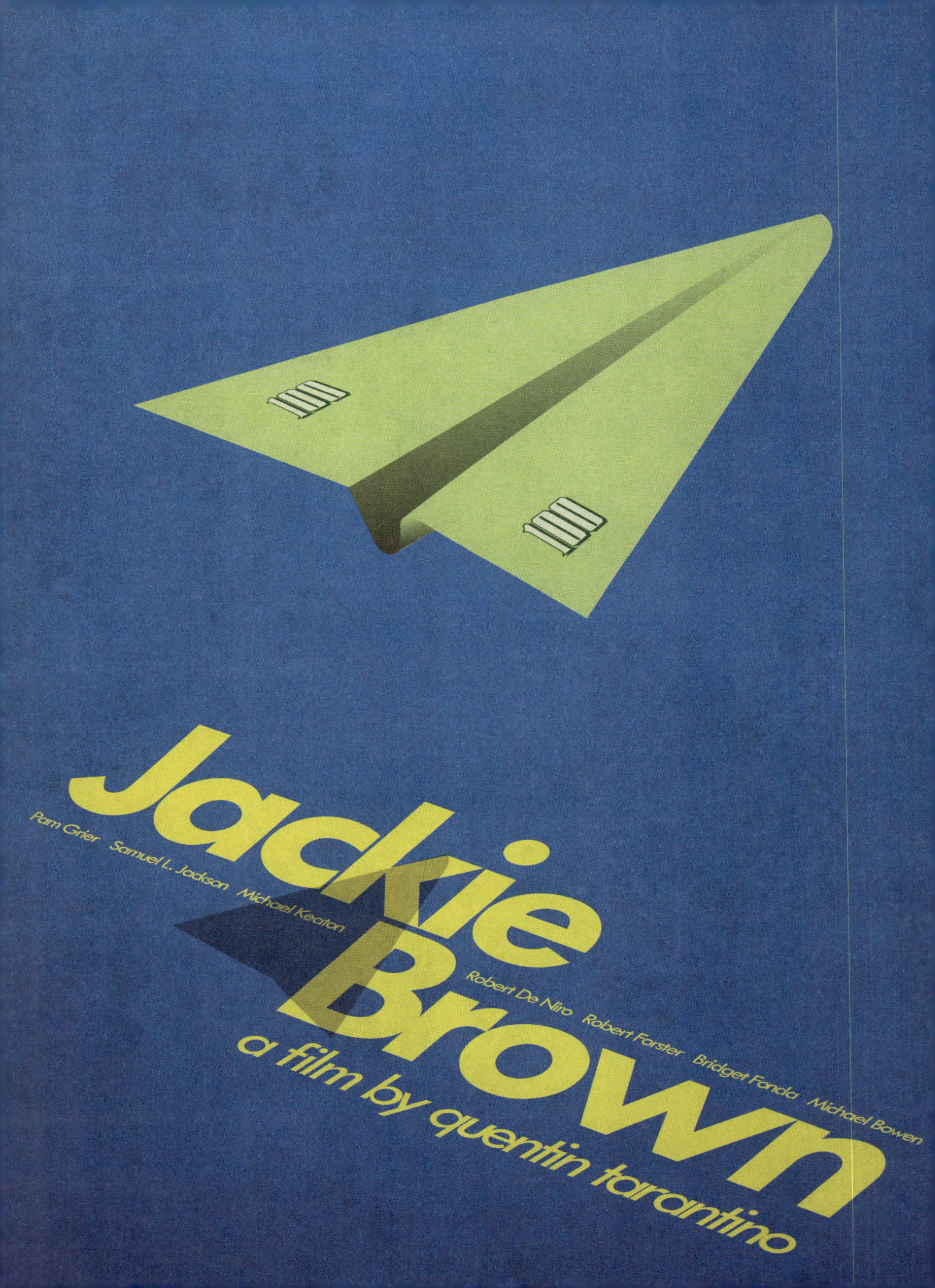
100
100
Jackie Brown
Pam Grier Samuel L. Jackson Michael Keaton
Robert De Niro Robert Forster Bridget Fonda Michael Bowen
a film by quentin tarantino

JACKIE BROWN

1997

Not everyone knows that Jackie Brown is the film adaptation of Elmore Leonard's novel Rum Punch (1992). The film differs from the rest of Tarantino's work and was criticised by some fans who missed a gooc dose of blood and violence, although it got very good reviews by critics.
The star, Pam Grier, had auditioned to play Jody in Pulp Fiction, but Tarantino chose Rosanna Arquette instead. However, the director did not forget the actress and decided to give her the lead role of Jackie Brown.

No todo el mundo sabe que Jackie Brown es la adaptación cinematográfica de la novela Rum Punch (1992) escrita por Elmore Leonard. La pelicula difiere del resto de la filmografía y fue criticada por algunos seguidores que echaron de menos una buena dosis de violencia y sangre, aunque fue muy bien recibida por parte de los críticos.
La protagonista, Pam Grier, había hecho el casting para interpretar al personaje de Jody en Pulp Fiction, pero Tarantino eligió a Rosanna Arquette en su lugar. Sin embargo, el director no se olvidó de la actriz y decidió darle el papel principal de Jackie Brown.

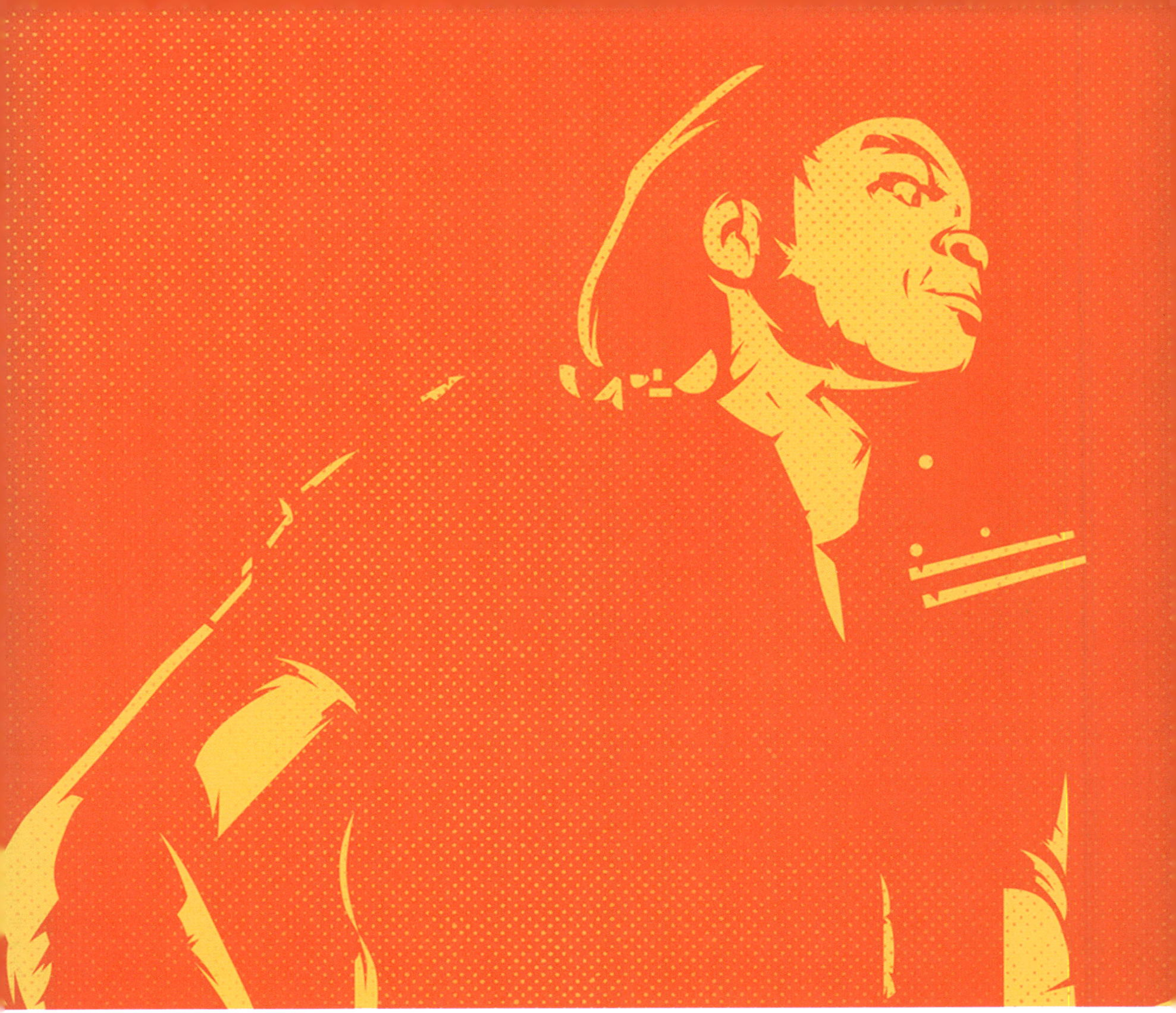

"Man, you must be out of your fuckin' mind if you think I'm gonna get in this dirty-ass trunk"

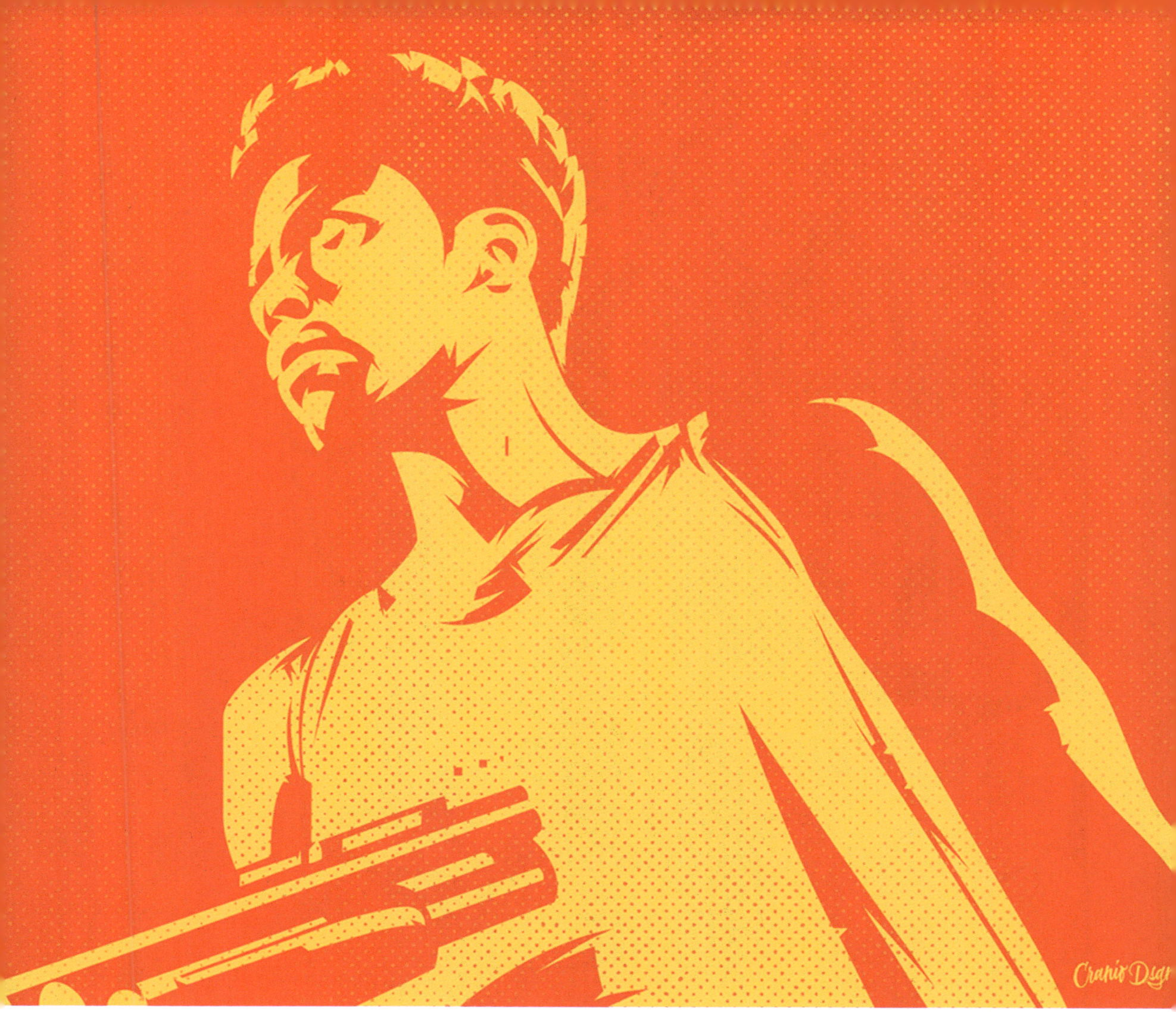

"Oye, debes estar completamente loco si crees que voy a meterme en ese asqueroso maletero"

- Beaumont Livingston -

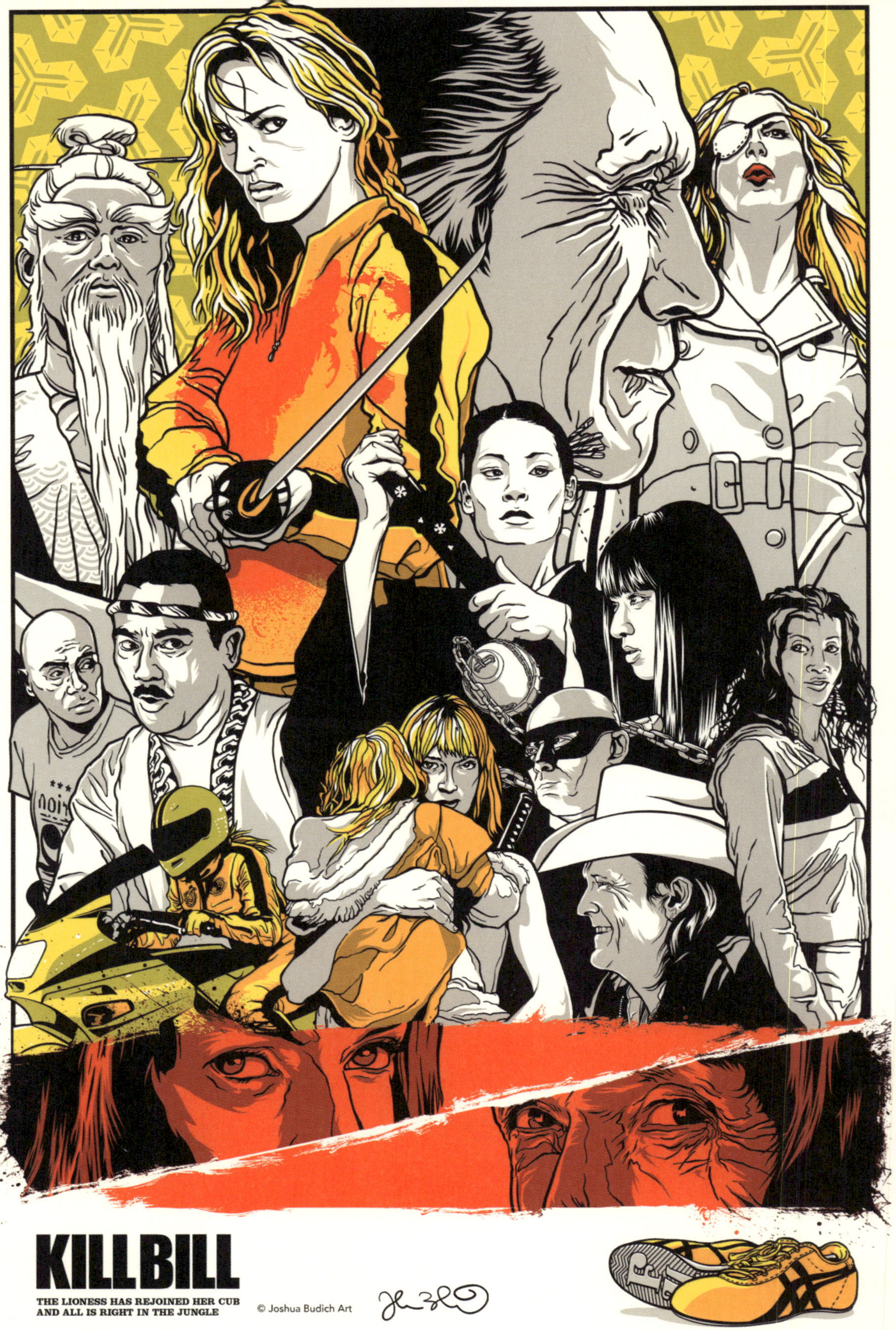
KILL BILL
THE LIONESS HAS REJOINED HER CUB
AND ALL IS RIGHT IN THE JUNGLE
© Joshua Budich Art

KILL BILL I-II

2003-2004

Tarantino and Uma Thurman say that Kill Bill was created during the filming of Pulp Fiction in 1994. They both fantasised about the kinds of films they would like to make. Tarantino said he wanted to make a 1970s kung-fu film, while the actress imagined herself dressed as a bride being shot, a sequence she would later immortalise in the film. Tarantino gave Thurman the script as a gift for her 30th birthday, along with the main role.

The yellow suit worn by the protagonist is the same as the one worn by Bruce Lee in his last film, "Game of Death" (1978).

Tarantino y Uma Thurman cuentan que Kill Bill se gestó durante el rodaje de Pulp Fiction en 1994. Ambos fantaseaban con los tipos de películas que les gustaría hacer. Tarantino dijo que quería hacer una cinta de kung-fu de los 70, mientras que la actriz se imaginó vestida de novia siendo disparada, secuencia que más tarde inmortalizaría en el filme. Tarantino le regaló el guión a Thurman como regalo para su 30 cumpleaños, así como el papel principal.

El traje amarillo que usa la protagonista es igual al que lleva Bruce Lee en su última película, "Juego con la muerte" (1978).

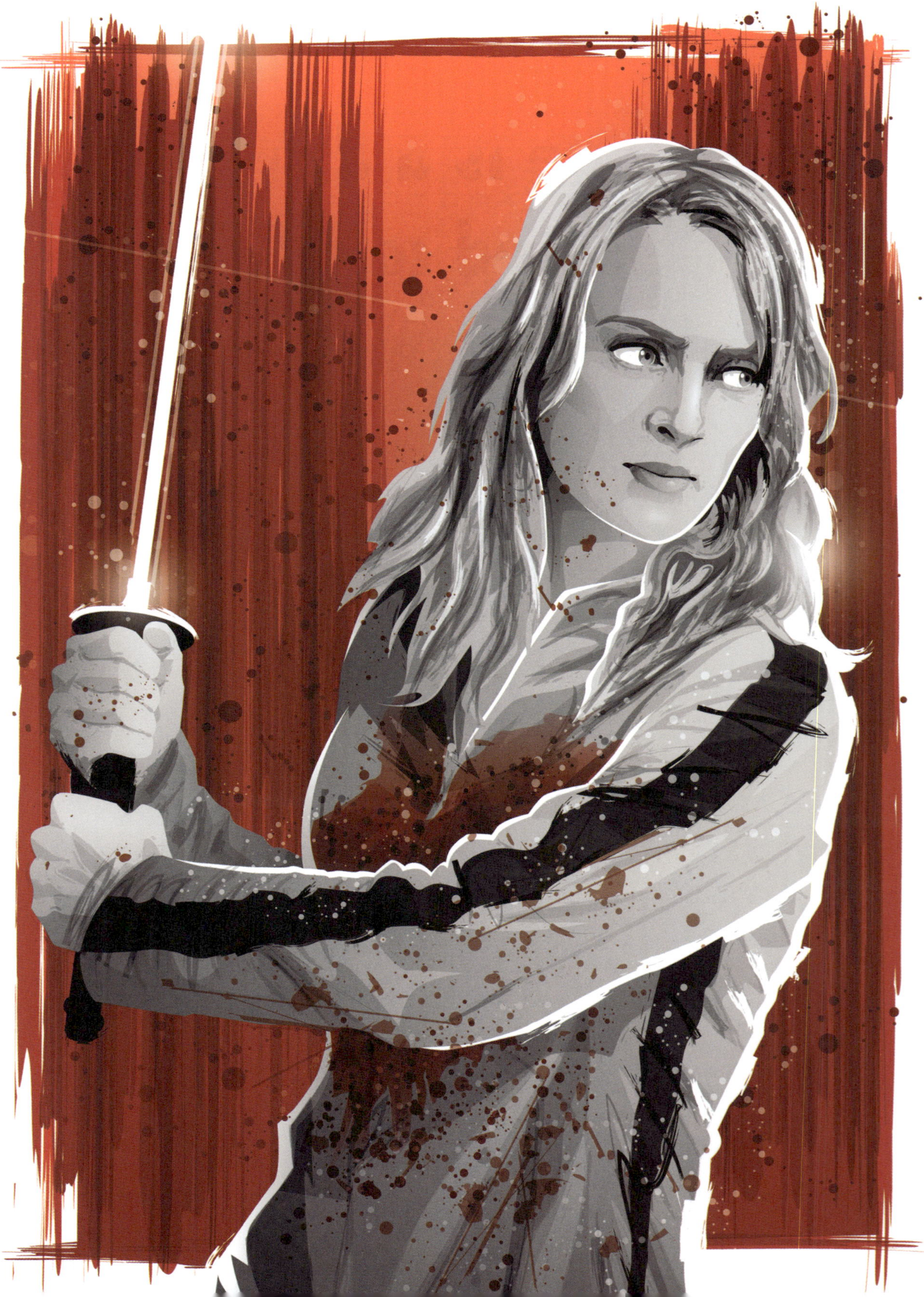

"Revenge is a dish best served cold"

"La venganza es un plato que sabe mejor si se sirve frío"

Hattori Hanzō

Hattori Hanzō was a samurai from the Sengoku and Azuchi-Momoyama periods of Japanese history. He is also considered one of the best-known ninjas and leader of the Iga clans.

He and his men were responsible for the security of Edo Castle, one of whose gates was named after him, and continues to bear his name today.

He died in 1596. It is believed that he was killed by a rival ninja named Fuma Kotaro.

Hattori Hanzō fue un samurai de los periodos Sengoku y Azuchi-Momoyama de la historia de Japón. También se le considera uno de los ninja más conocidos, y líder de los clanes de Iga.

Él y sus hombres eran los encargados de velar por la seguridad del Castillo Edo, de la que una puerta fue nombrada con su nombre, algo que perdura hasta el día de hoy.

Murió en 1596. Se cree que fue asesinado por un ninja rival llamado Fuma Kotaro.

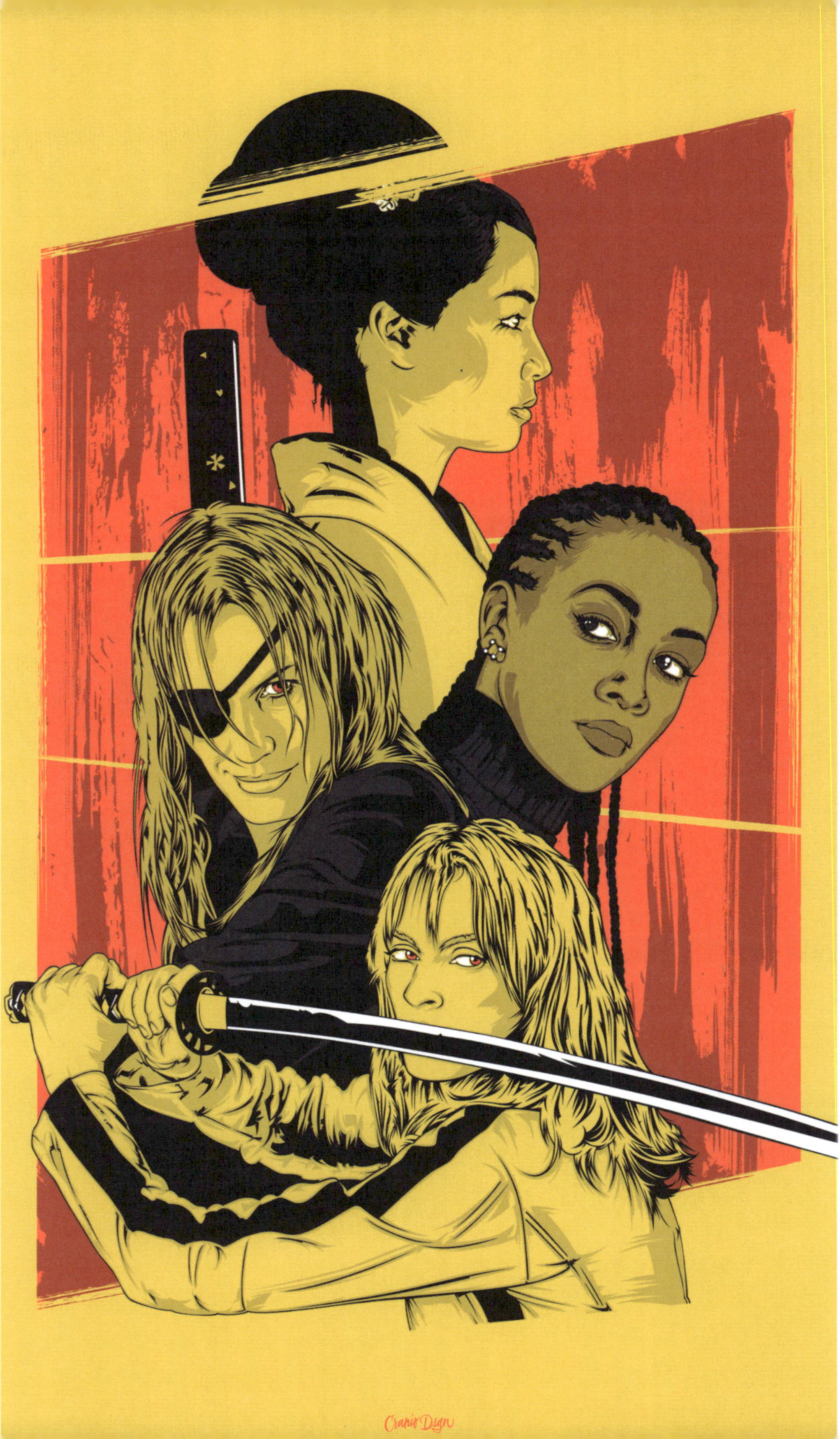
Cranio Dsgn

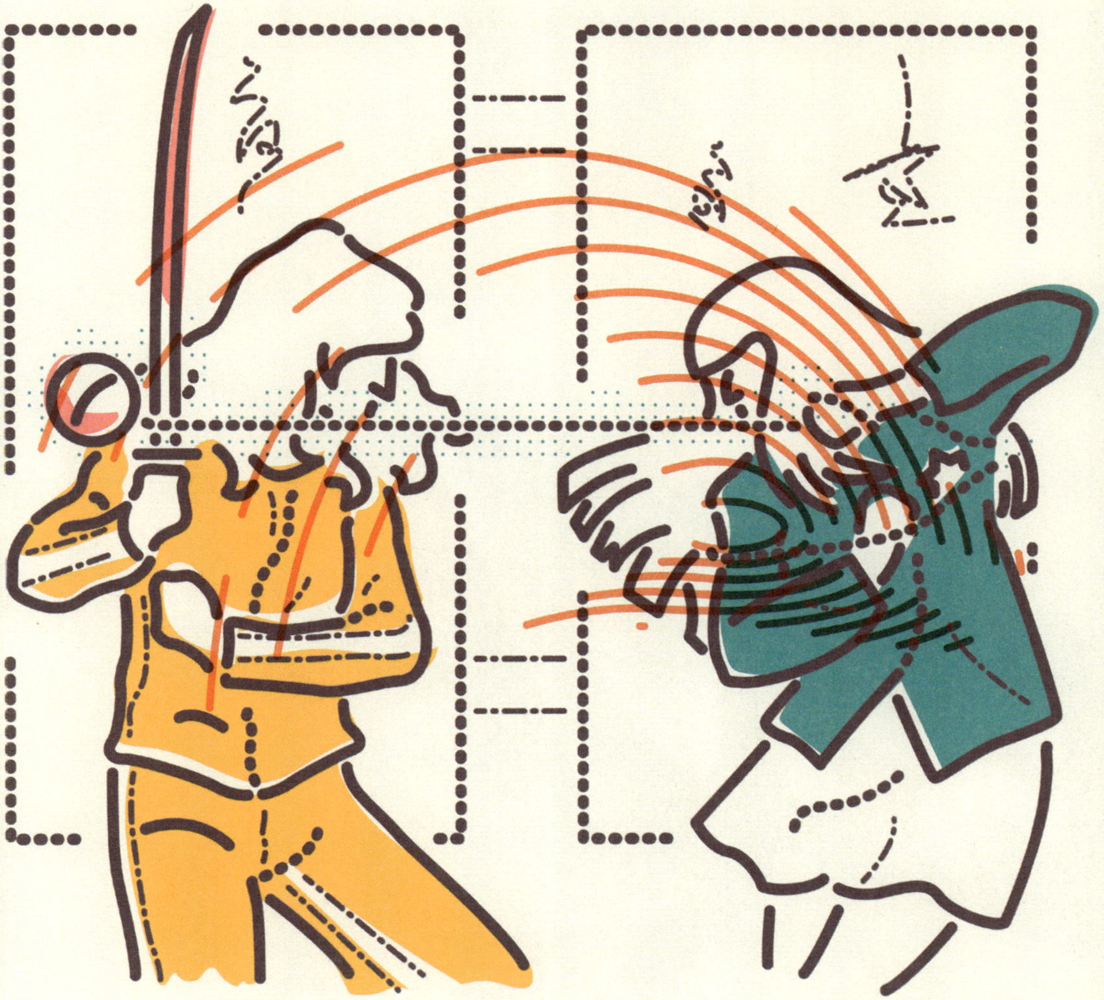

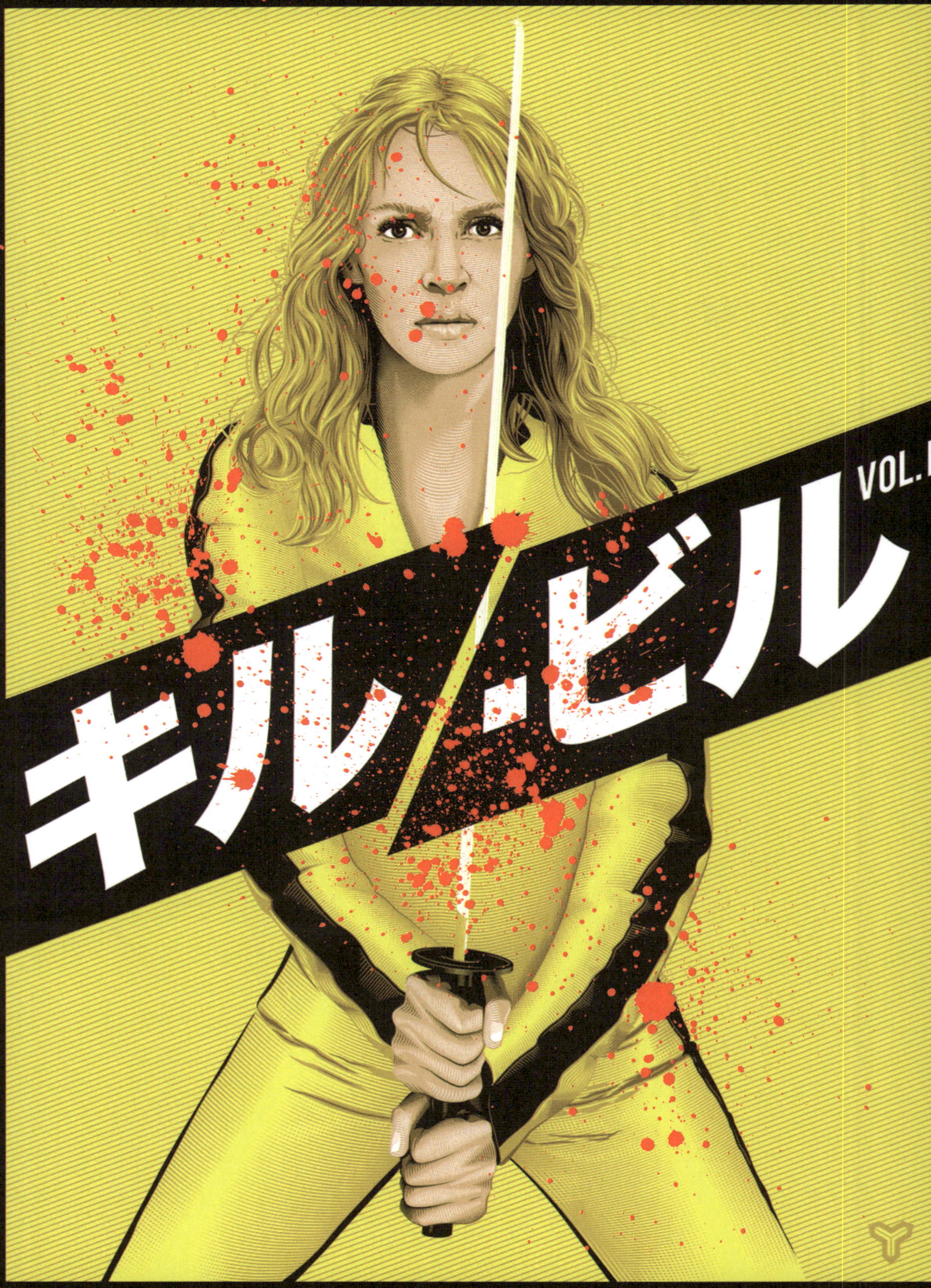
VOL. I
キル・ビル

"Those of you lucky enough to have your lives, take them with you. However, leave the limbs you've lost. They belong to me now"

"Los que tengáis la suerte de seguir con vida podéis iros. Pero dejad aquí vuestros miembros cercenados. Ahora me pertenecen"

- Black Mamba -

O-Ren Ishii

O-Ren Ishii was born on an American military base in Tokyo. At the age of 9, while hiding under her bed, she witnessed the brutal murder of her parents by Matsumoto, Japan's most ruthless Yakuza chief.

O-Ren swore revenge, and at the age of 11, taking advantage of the fact that Matsumoto was a paedophile, used his catana against him, and shot his bodyguards.

At the age of 20 she was one of the world's biggest killers. It was then that Bill called her to form part of his "Lethal Viper Killer Squad". Her code name was Cotton Mouth. At the age of 25 she participated in the murder of 9 innocent people including the daughter of the Bride.

O-Ren Ishii nació en una base militar americana en Tokio, a los 9 años es testigo del brutal asesinato de sus padres, a manos de Matsumoto, el jefe Yakuza más despiadado de Japón, mientras ella estaba escondida bajo la cama.

O-Ren juró vengarse, y a los 11 años, aprovechando que Matsumoto era pederasta, utilizó contra él su catana, y disparó a sus guardaespaldas.

A los 20 años era ya una de las mayores asesinas del mundo. Fue entonces cuando Bill la llamó para formar parte de su "Escuadrón Asesino Víbora Letal". Su nombre clave fue Mocasín (Cotton Mouth en el original). A los 25 años participó en el asesinato de 9 personas inocentes incluida la hija de la Novia.

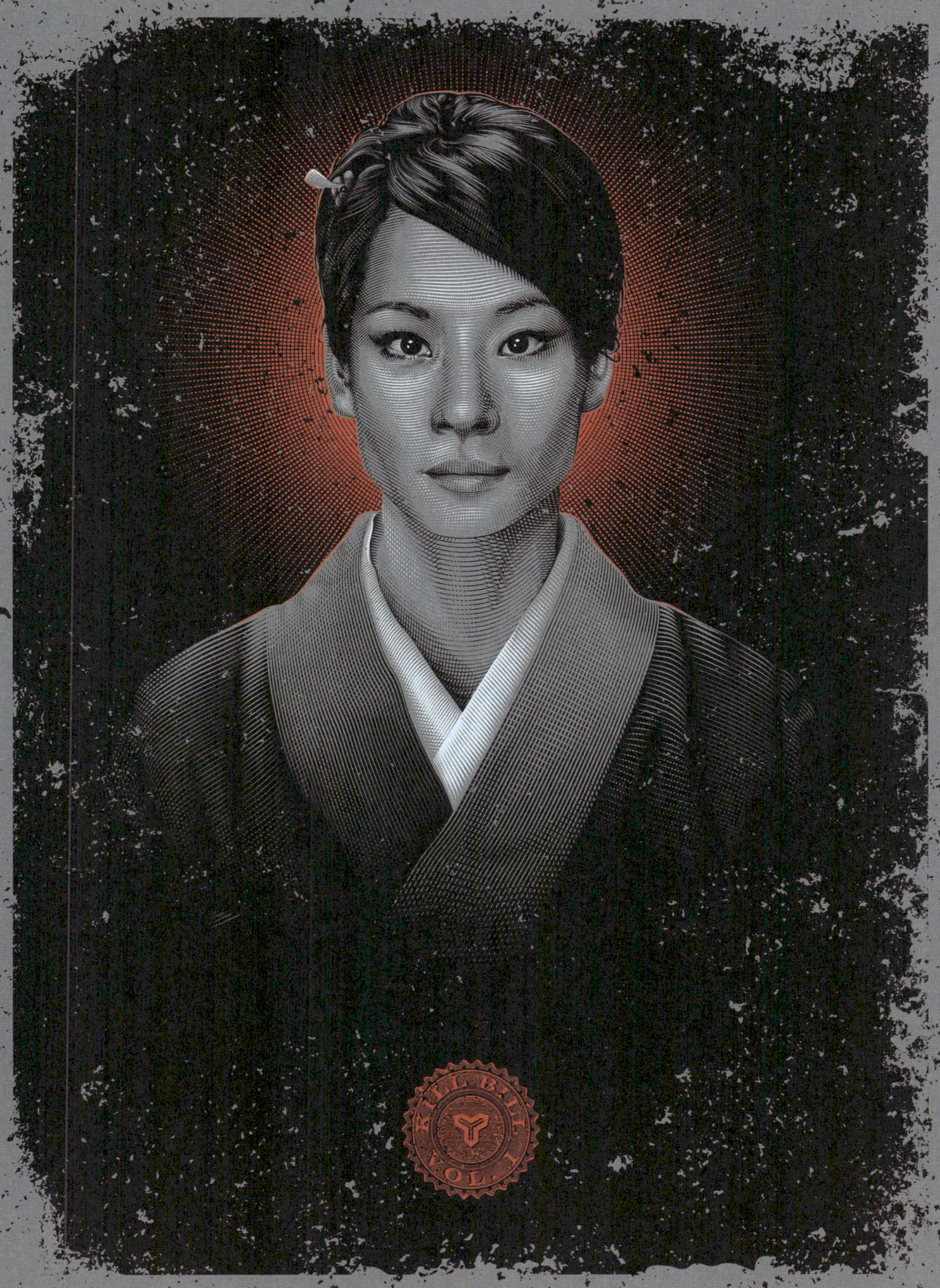
KILL BILL
VOL. 1

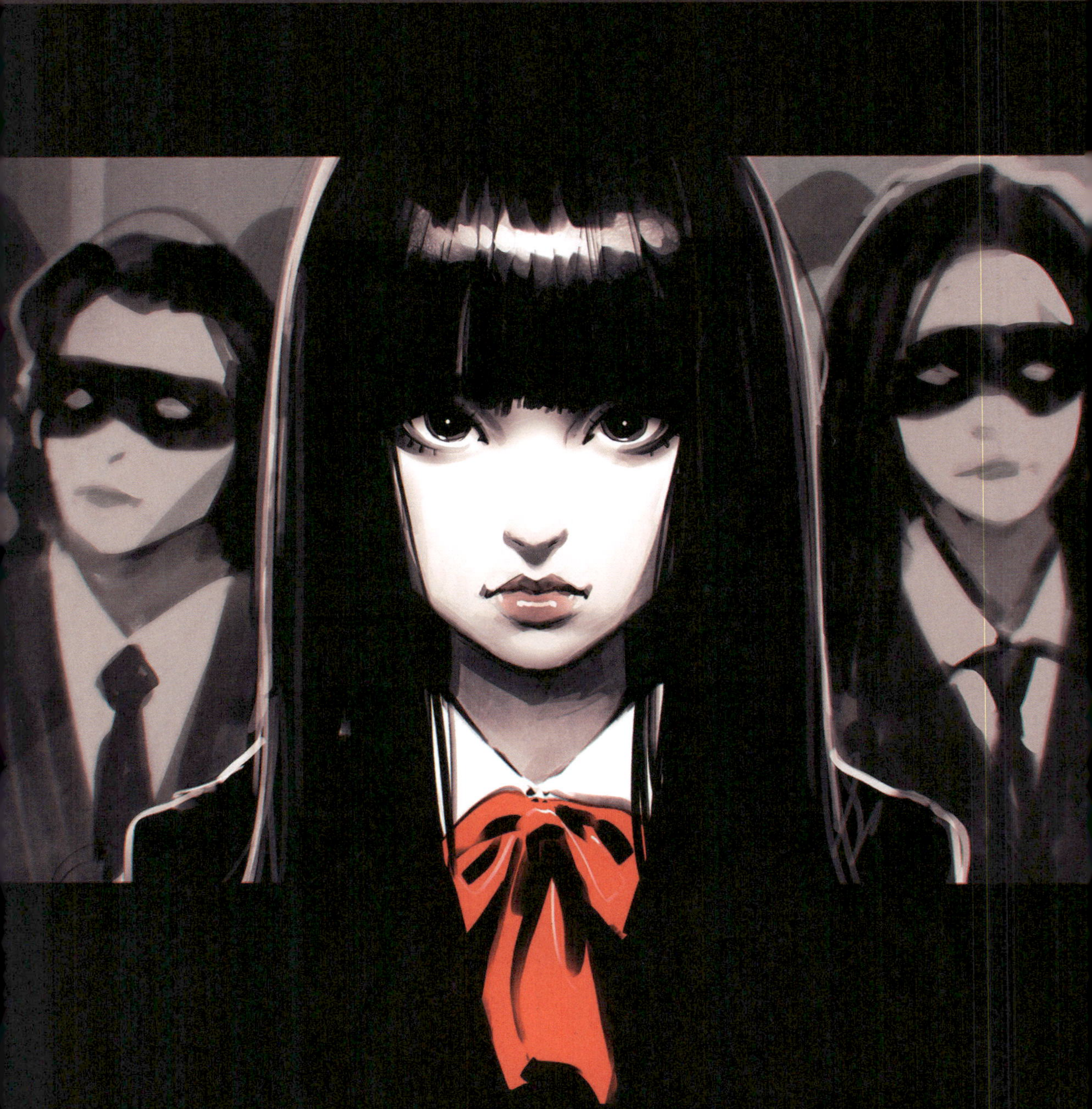

"You call that begging?... You can beg better than that"

"¿A eso llamas suplicar?...
puedes suplicar mucho mejor"

- Gogo Yubari -

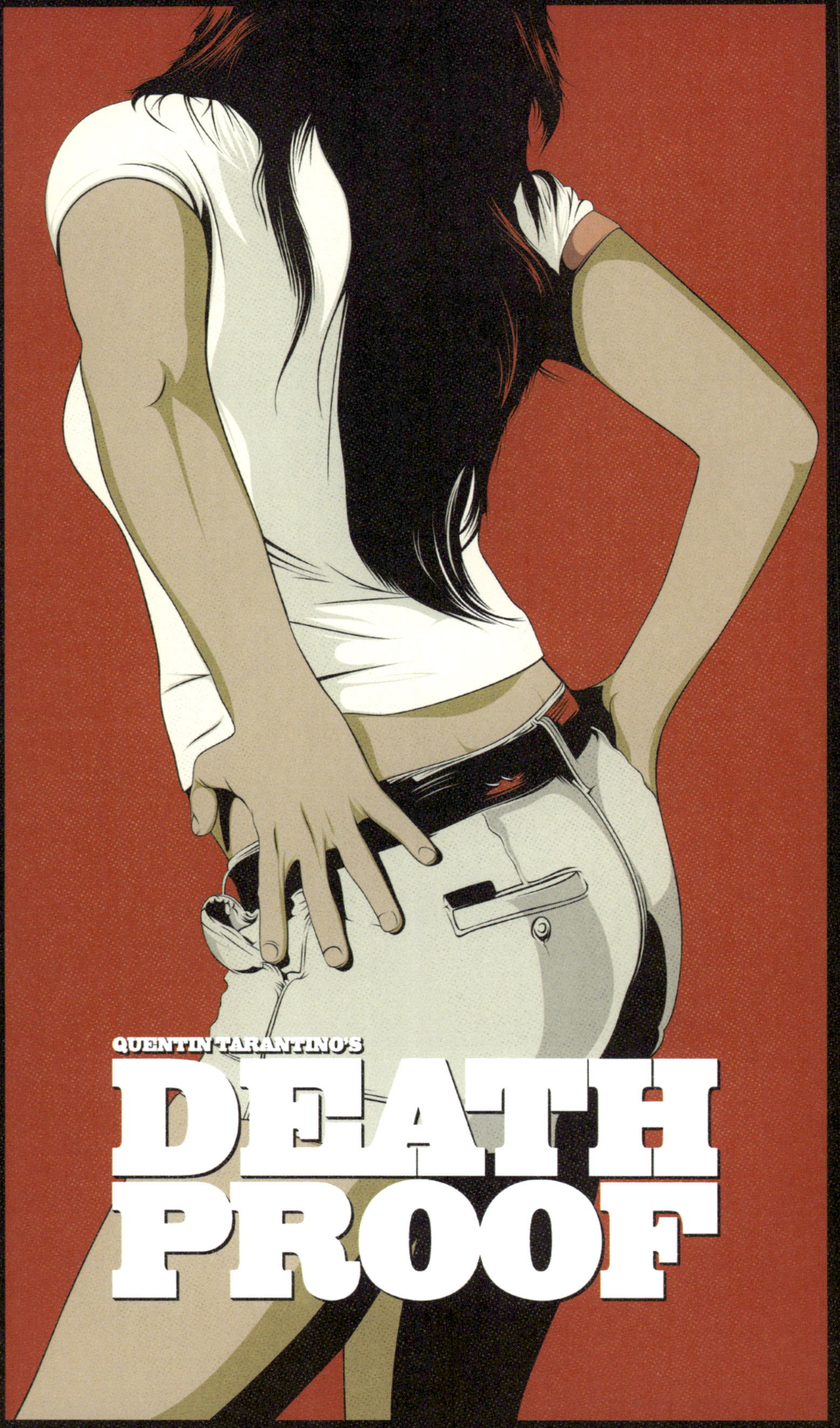
QUENTIN TARANTINO'S
DEATH
PROOF

DEATH PROOF 2007

Texas Chili Parlor

Austin TX

This is one of the most popular restaurants for lunch, located near the Texas City Government building. This is where all the characters from the first part of this spine-chilling thriller meet. Jungle Julia, Shanna and Arlene are waiting for a fourth friend to arrive so they can begin their holidays without realising they are being stalked by a very sinister guy. Jungle Julia confesses that that morning, on the radio, she had offered a sexy dance that Arlene would perform for the first person to call her "butterfly", buy her a drink and recite a certain fragment from a poem. Before they leave the bar, Stuntman Mike calls Arlen "butterfly".

Austin TX

Este es uno de los restaurantes favoritos para tomar el almuerzo, está ubicado cerca del edificio del Gobierno de la Ciudad de Texas. Aquí se reunen todos los personajes de la primera parte de este thriller escalofriante. Jungle Julia, Shanna y Arlene, esperan la llegada de una cuarta amiga para poder iniciar sus vacaciones, sin darse cuenta que están siendo acechadas por un tipo muy siniestro. Jungle Julia confiesa que esa mañana ofreció por la radio un baile sexy que realizaría Arlene a la primera persona que la llame "mariposa", le compre una bebida y le recite un fragmento de un poema. Antes de que estas se vayan del bar, el especialista Mike llamará "mariposa" a Arlen.

"This car is 100% death proof, but to get the benefit of it honey, you really need to be sittin' in MY seat!"

"Este coche es a prueba de muerte 100%, pero nena, para sacarle todo el partido, hay que estar en MI asiento"

- Stuntman Mike -

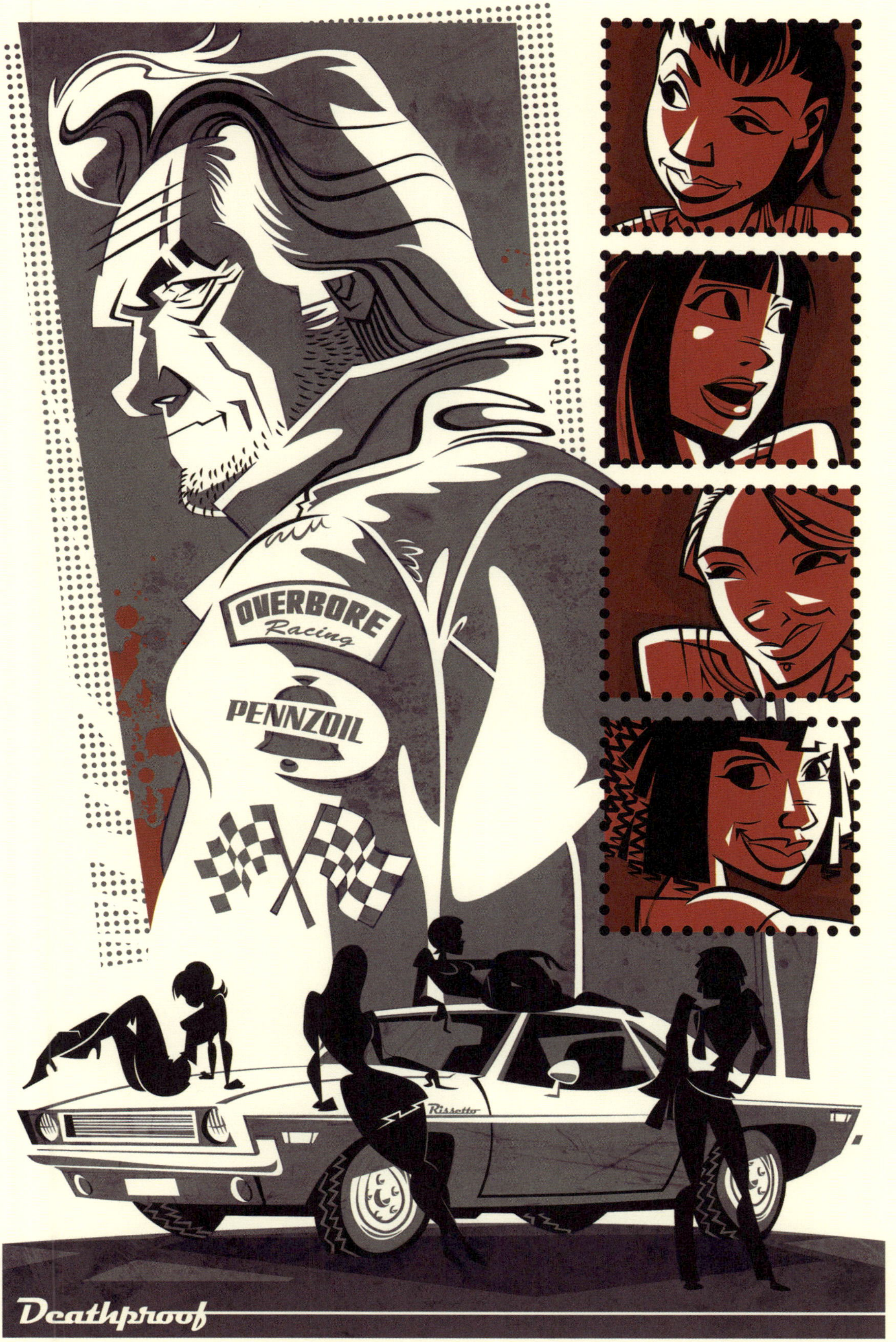
OVERBORE
Racing
PENNZOIL
Rissetto
Deathproof

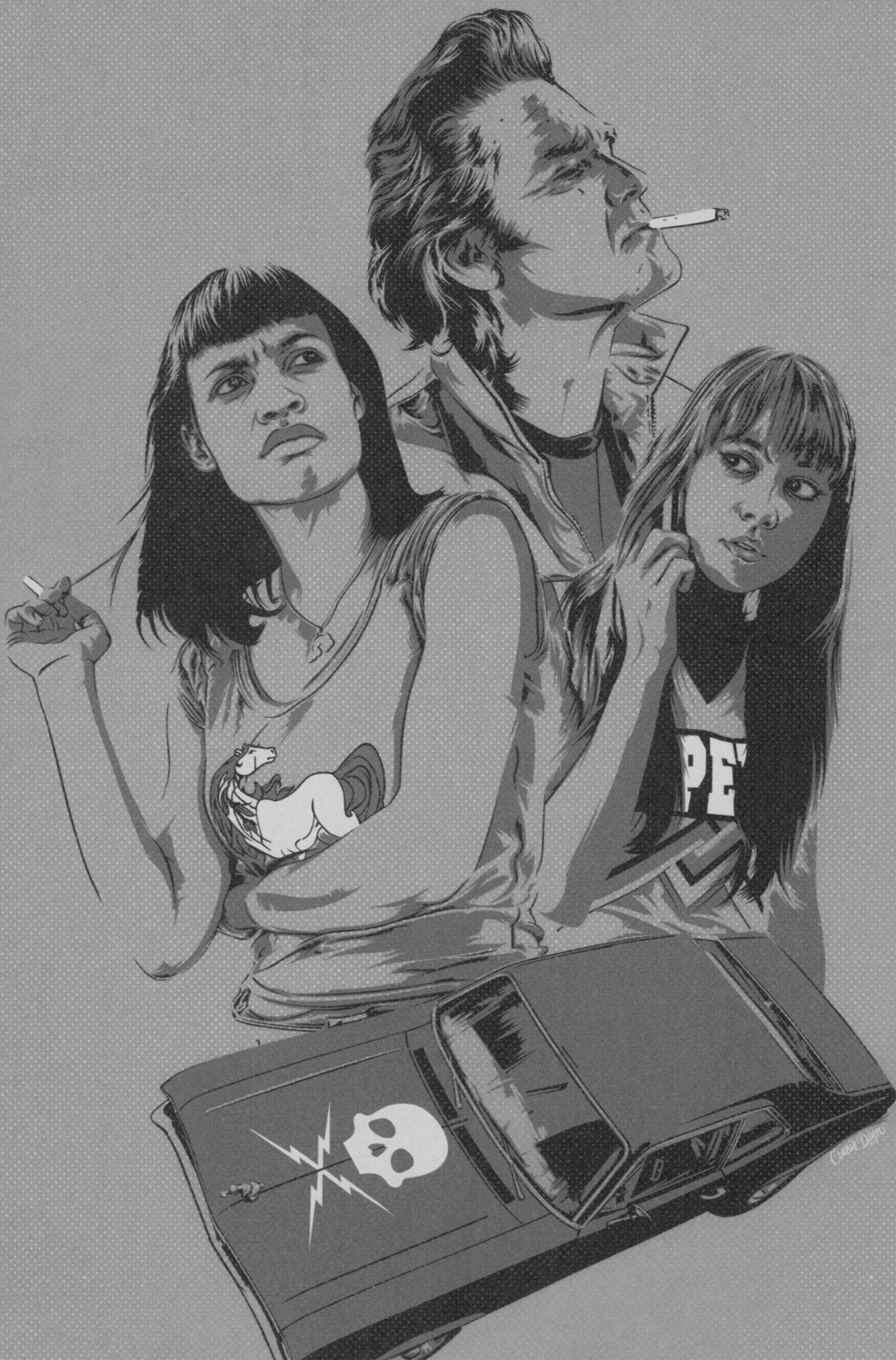
PET

"I'm not a cowboy, Pam... I'm a stuntman"

"No soy un vaquero Pam...
Soy un especialista"

- Stuntman Mike -

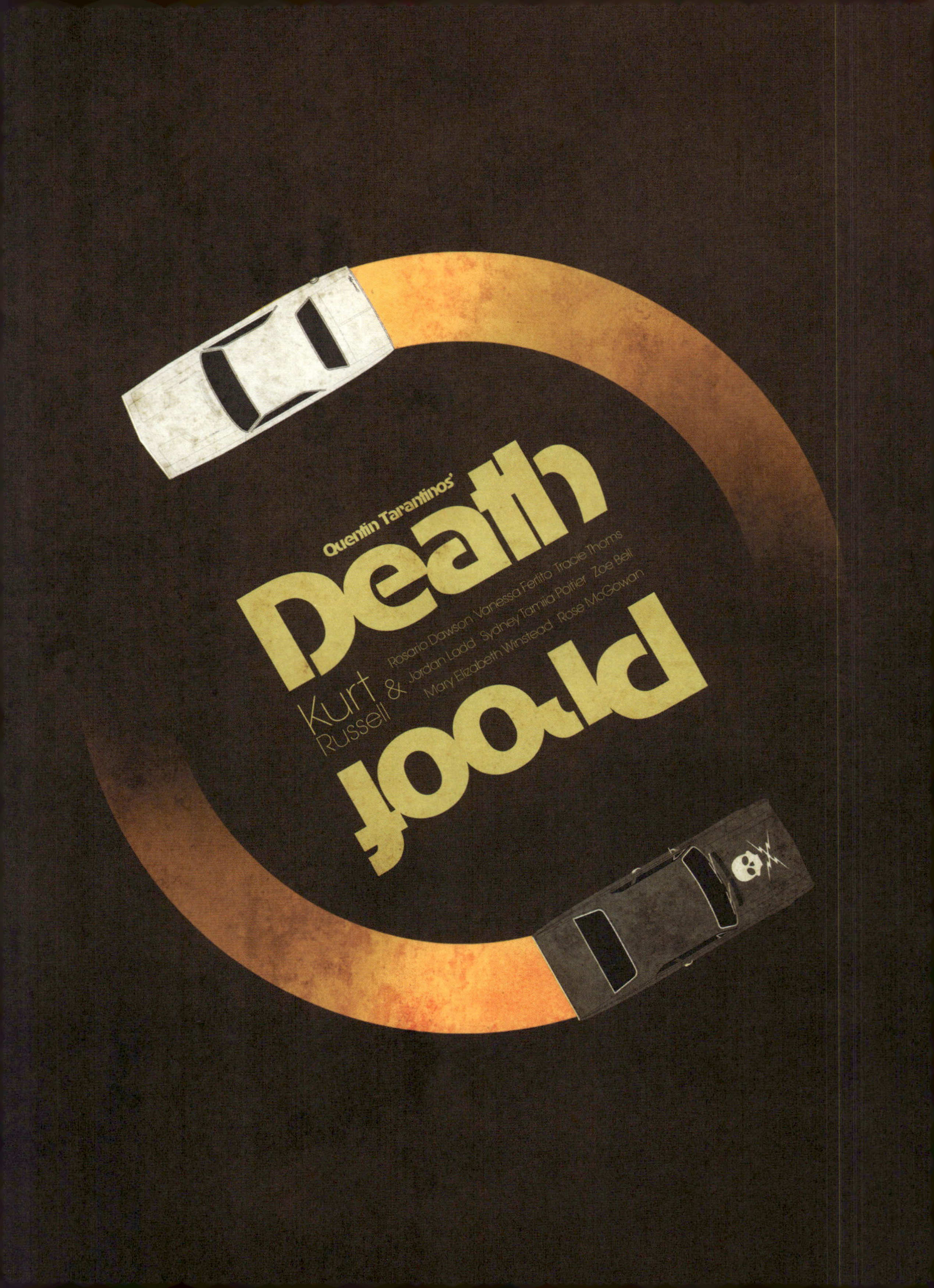
Quentin Tarantinos'
Death
Proof
Kurt Russell &
Rosario Dawson Vanessa Ferlito Tracie Thoms
Jordan Ladd Sydney Tamiia Poitier Zoe Bell
Mary Elizabeth Winstead Rose McGowan

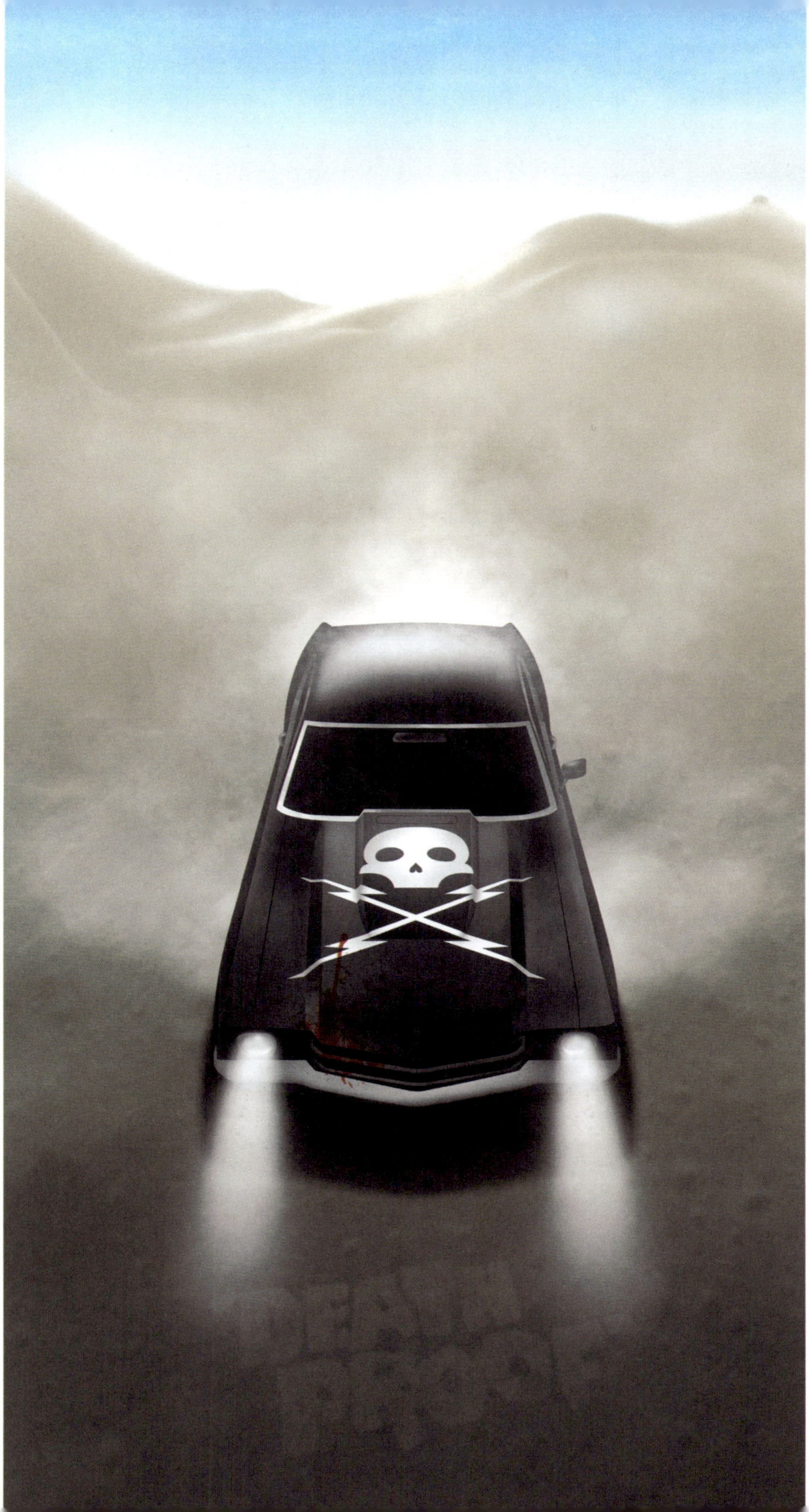

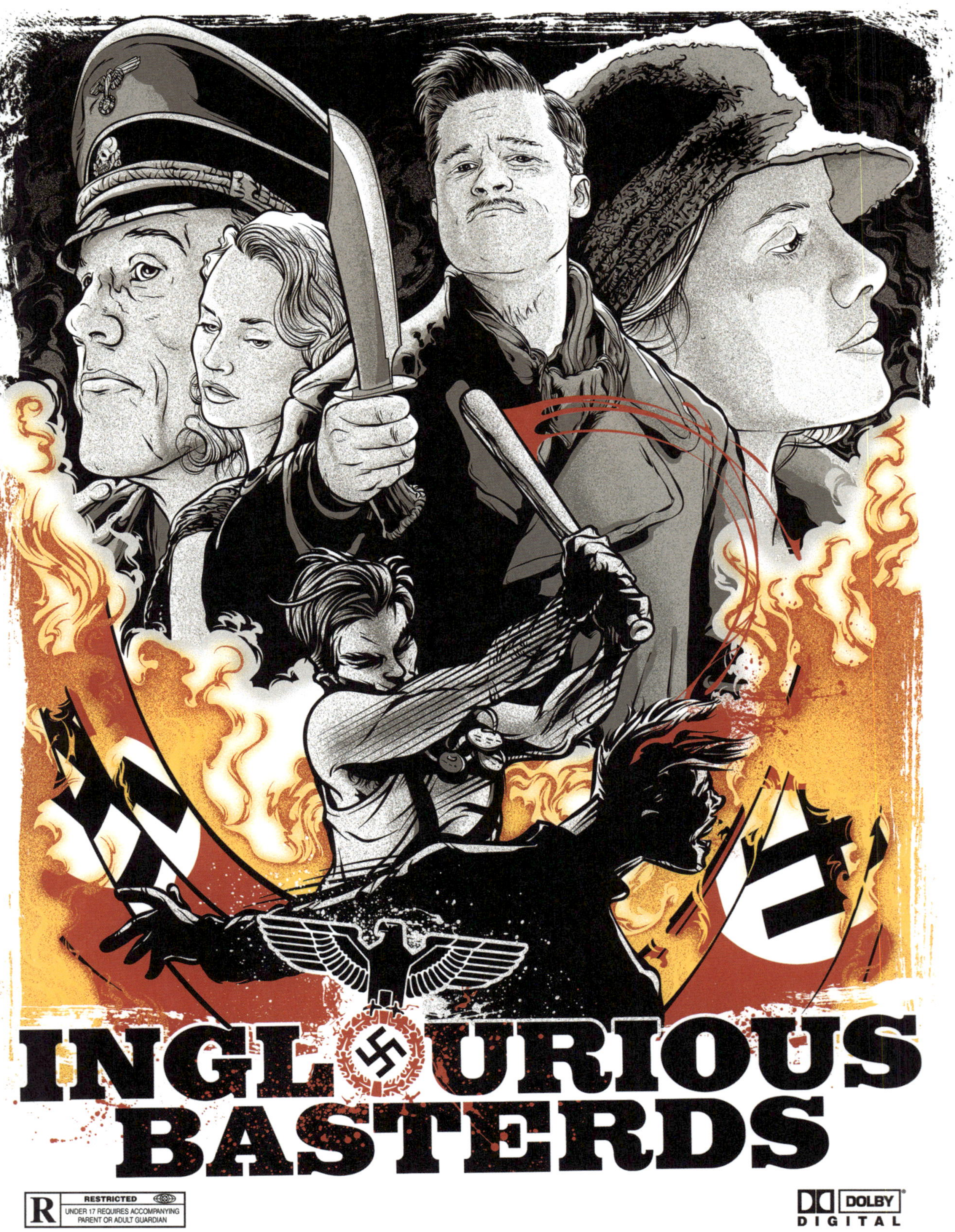
INGLOURIOUS
BASTERDS
R
RESTRICTED
UNDER 17 REQUIRES ACCOMPANYING
PARENT OR ADULT GUARDIAN
DOLBY
DIGITAL

INGLORIOUS BASTERDS

2009

Tarantino had countless ideas for this film, and the original script underwent several changes, so much so that he wrote 3 separate scripts before completing the final one on 2 July 2008.

The film gets its title from the Italian film "Quel maledetto treno blindato", directed by Enzo Castellari in 1978, which in English was called "Inglorious Bastards". Tarantino himself said that the mystery of why he decided to use the spelling "basterds" instead of "bastards" will never be revealed, and that in fact "it makes it more interesting". The director confesses that what he likes most about this film is "The idea that the strength of the film industry serves to fight the Nazis, and I don't mean metaphorically, but literally".

Tarantino tenía infinidad de ideas para esta película, y el guión original sufrió varios cambios desde que se inició, tanto es así que escribió 3 guiones independientes, hasta terminar el definitivo el 2 de julio de 2008.

La cinta obtiene su título de la película italiana "Quel maledetto treno blindato", dirigida por Enzo Castellari en 1978, y que en inglés se llamó "Inglorious bastards". El propio Tarantino dijo que el misterio de porqué usó "basterds" en lugar de "bastards" nunca será revelado, y que de hecho "lo hace más interesante". El director confiesa que lo que más le gusta de esta película es "La idea de que la fuerza del cine sirva para luchar contra los nazis, y no me refiero metafóricamente, sino de verdad".

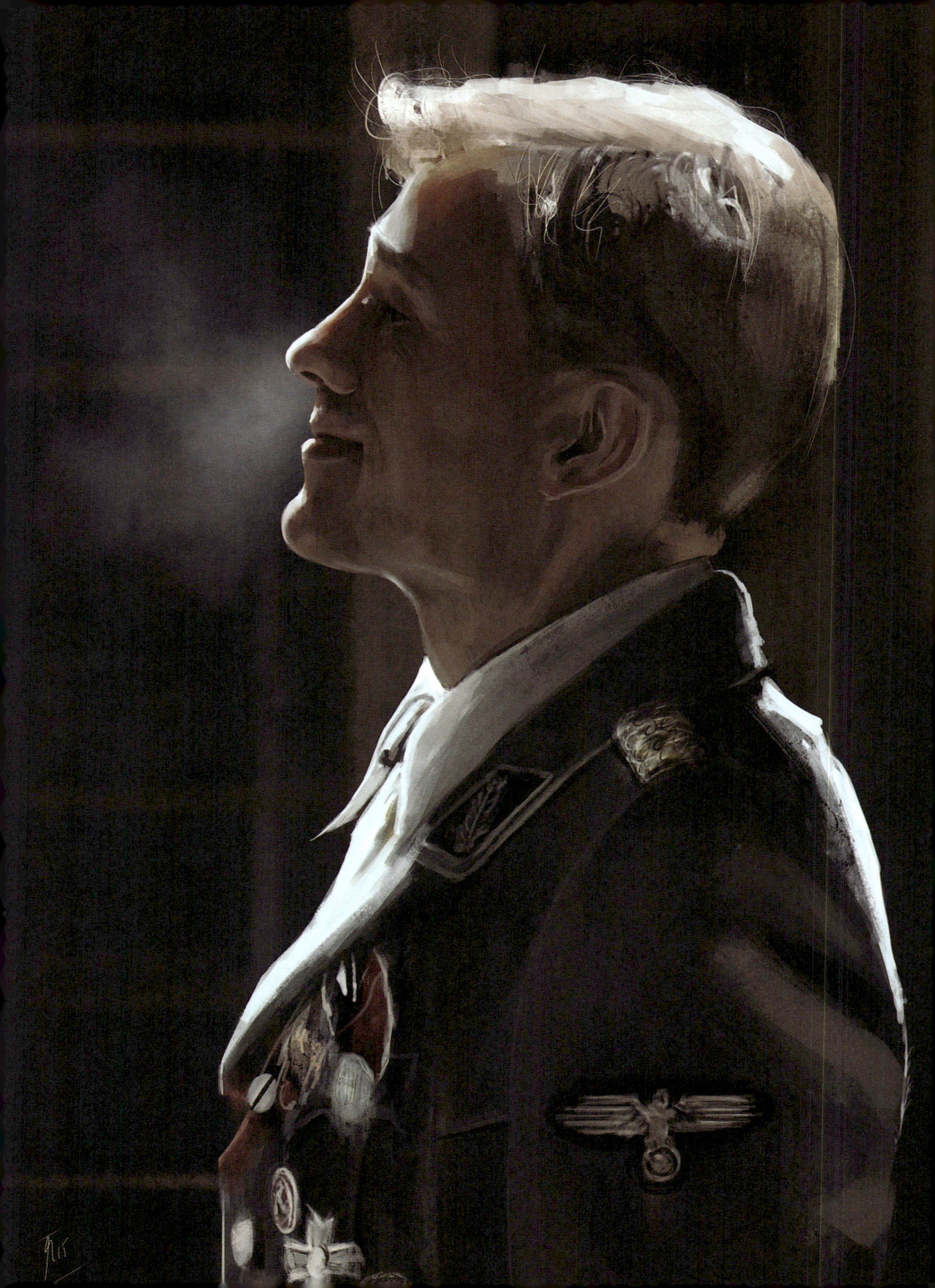

"Oooh, That's a Bingo!"

- Hans Landa -

Hans Landa

Merciless, arrogant, inhuman... and smart and polite at the same time. This is Hans Landa, nicknamed "the Jew Hunter", without a doubt, one of the greatest characters that Tarantino has ever created.

Despiadado, arrogante, inhumano... e inteligente y educado al mismo tiempo. Este es Hans Landa, apodado "el Cazajudíos", sin lugar a dudas, uno de los personajes más grandes que Tarantino ha creado.

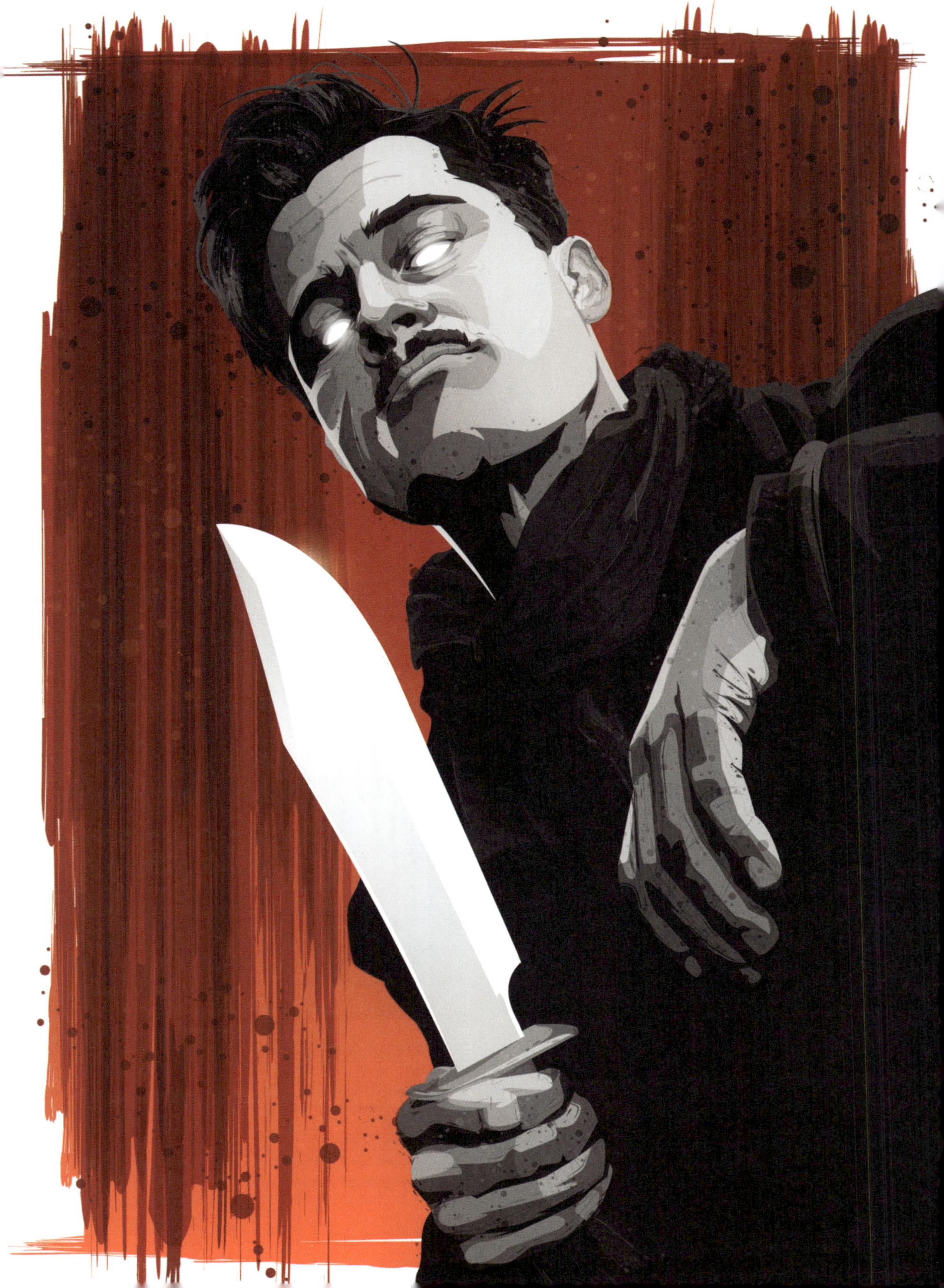

"Each and every man under my command owes me one hundred Nazi scalps. And I want my scalps!"

"Al entrar a esta unidad, cada uno de vosotros me debe un centenar de cabelleras nazis. ¡Y quiero esas cabelleras!"

- Aldo Raine -

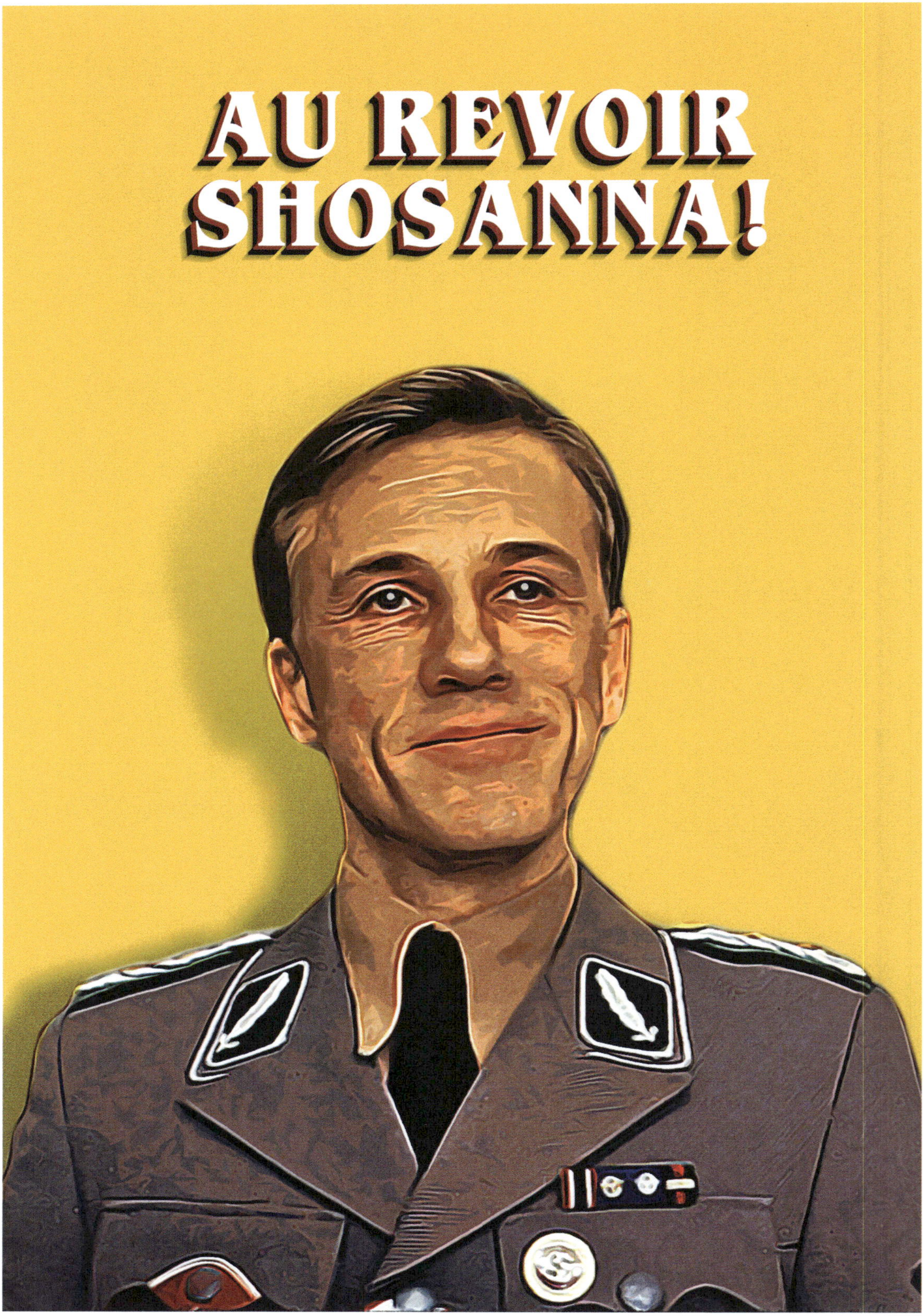
AU REVOIR
SHOSANNA!

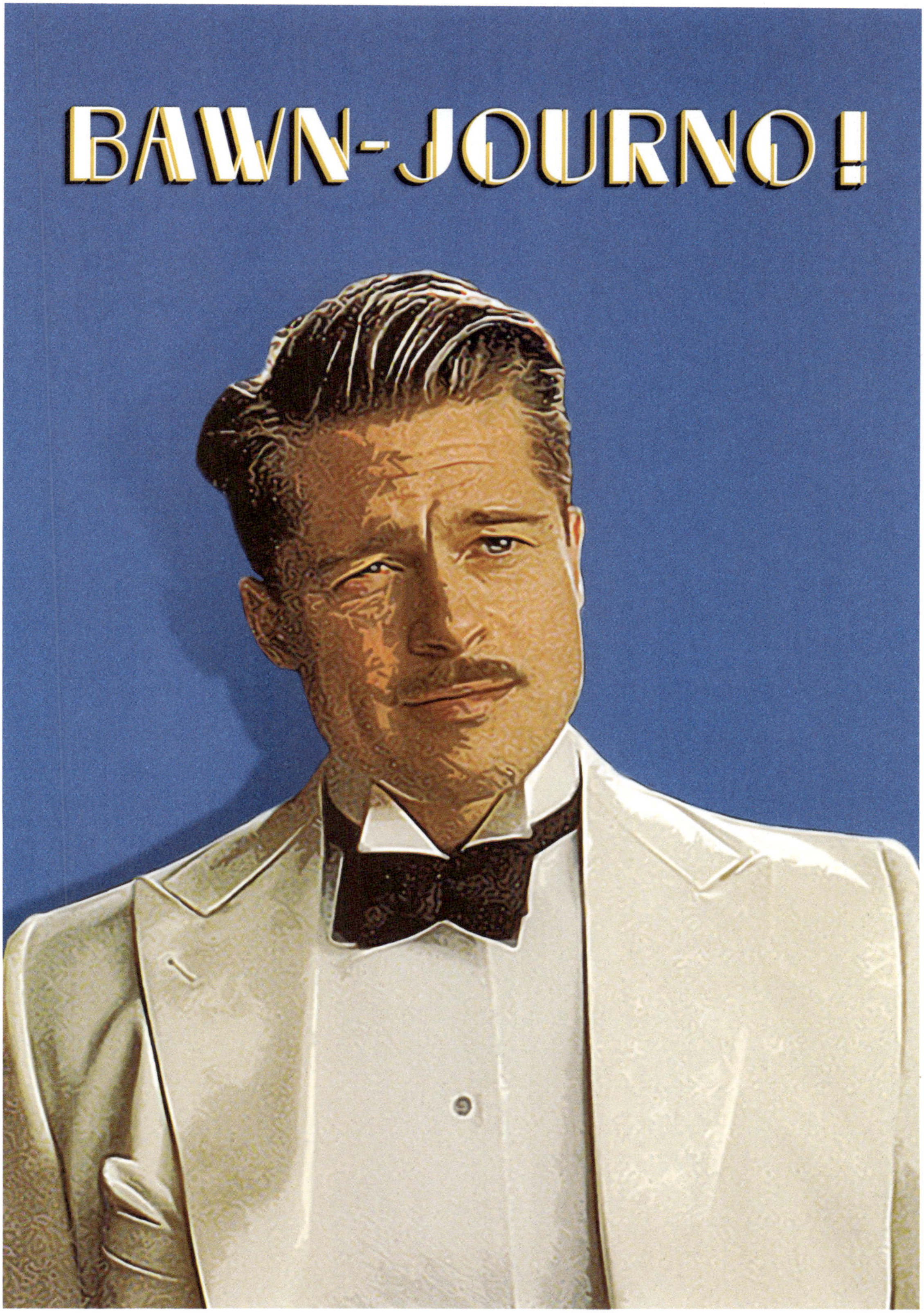
BAWN-JOURNO!

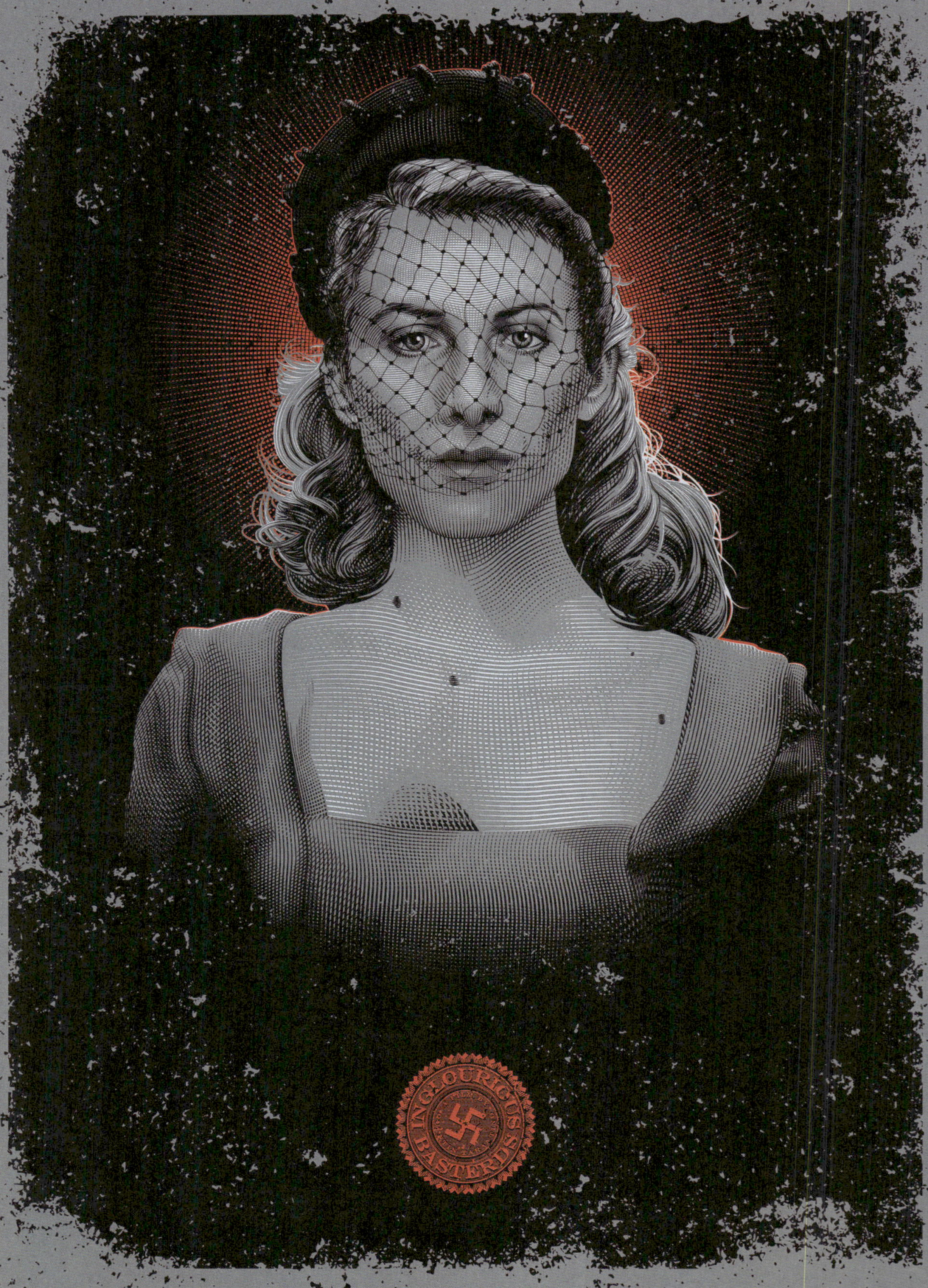
INGLOURIOUS
BASTERDS

"My name is Shosanna Dreyfus and this is the face... of Jewish vengeance!"

"Mi nombre es Shosanna Dreyfus
y este es el rostro de la venganza judía"

- Shosanna Dreyfus -

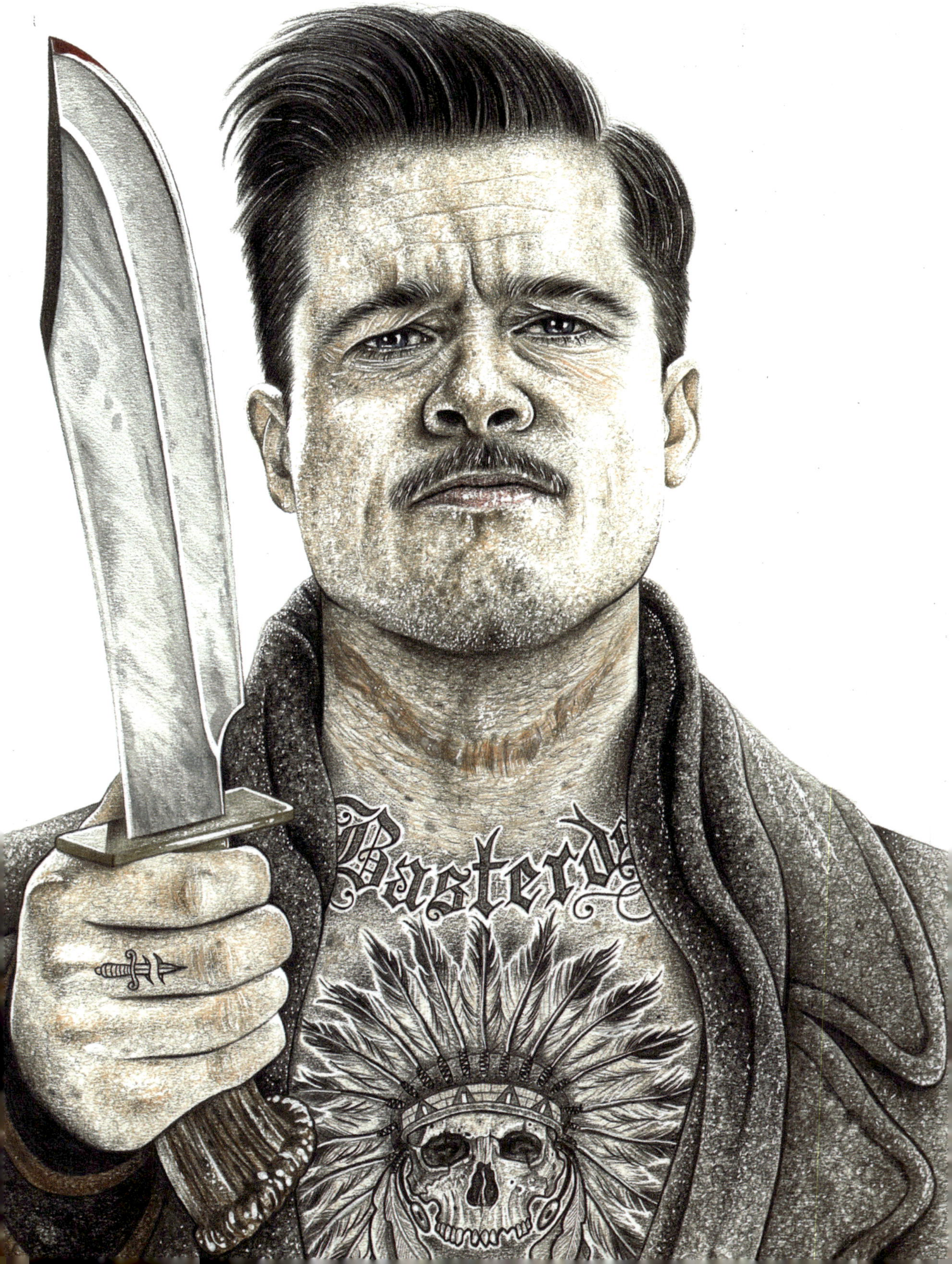
Basterd

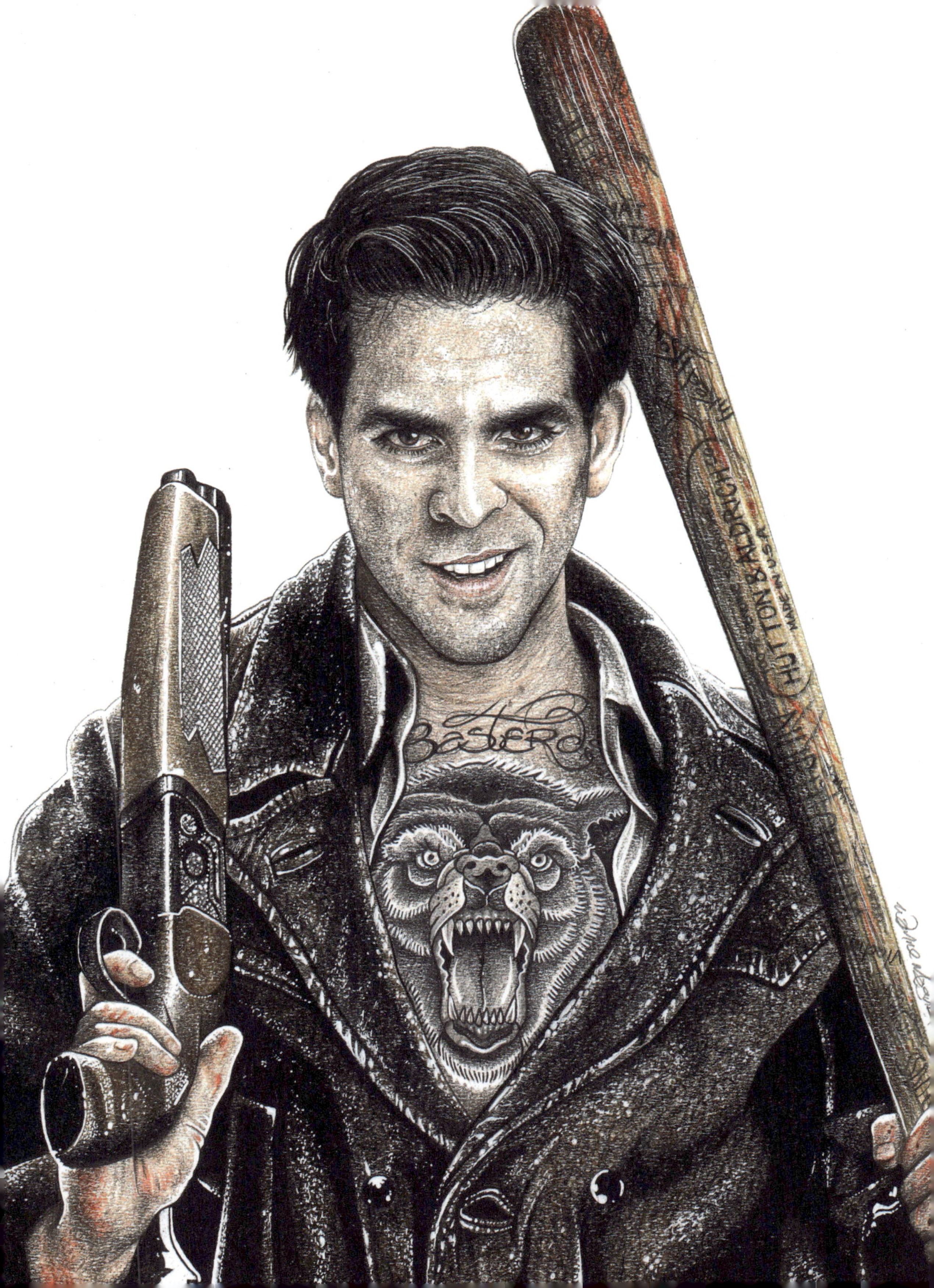
HUTTON & ALDRICH
MADE IN USA

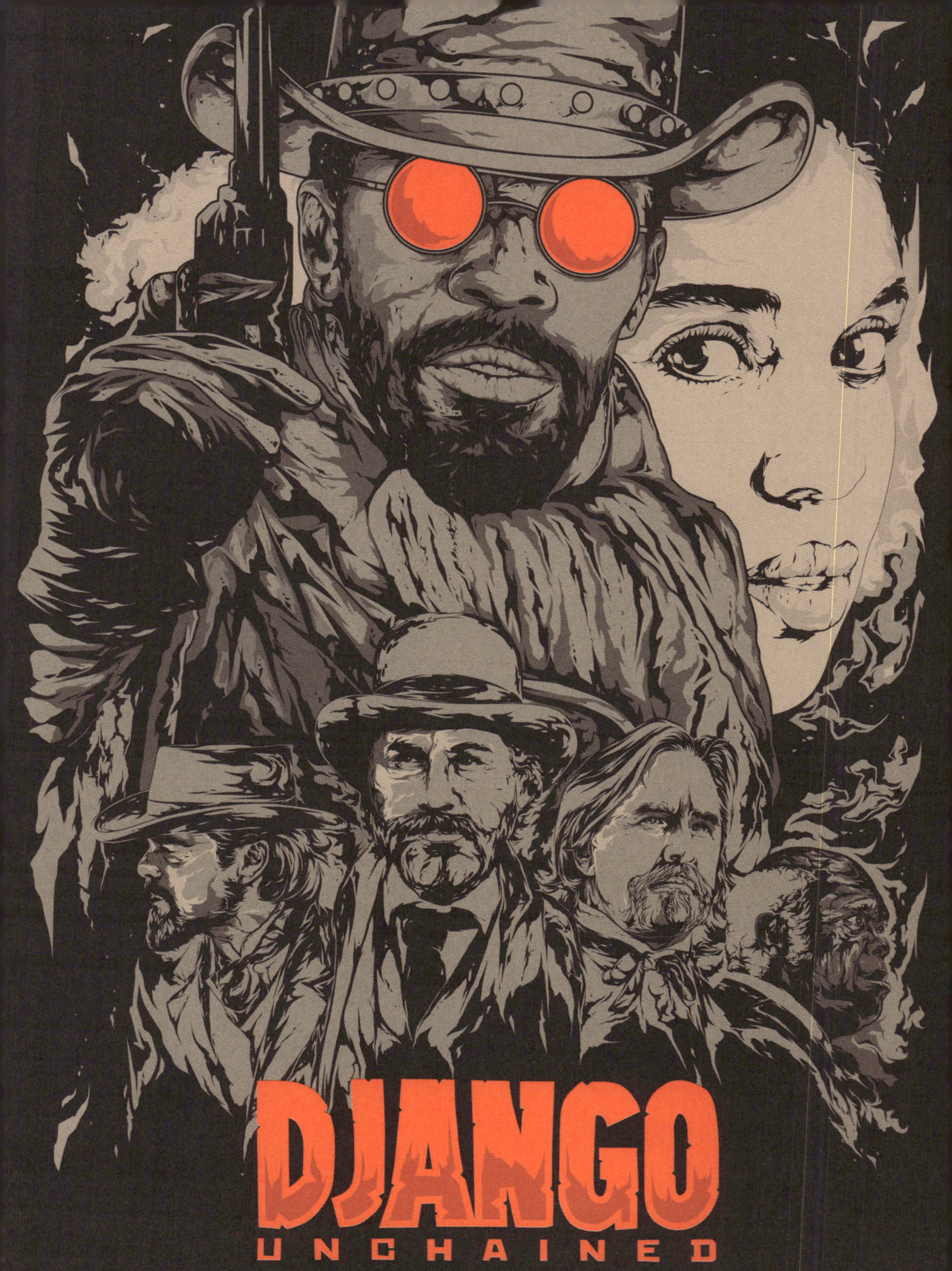

Poster Art by Harry Grundmann

DJANGO UNCHAINED

2012

Classical movies and especially Westerns are one of Tarantino's favourite film genres, his first film of this genre being "Django Unchained". It received so many positive reviews that a few years later the director decided to make a film with a similar atmosphere, "The Hateful Eight".

El cine clásico y en especial el Western es uno de los universos cinematográficos favoritos de Tarantino, su primer film de este género fue "Django Desencadenado". Las críticas positivas fueron tales, que unos años más tarde el director decidió embarcarse en una atmósfera similar con "Los Odiosos Ocho".

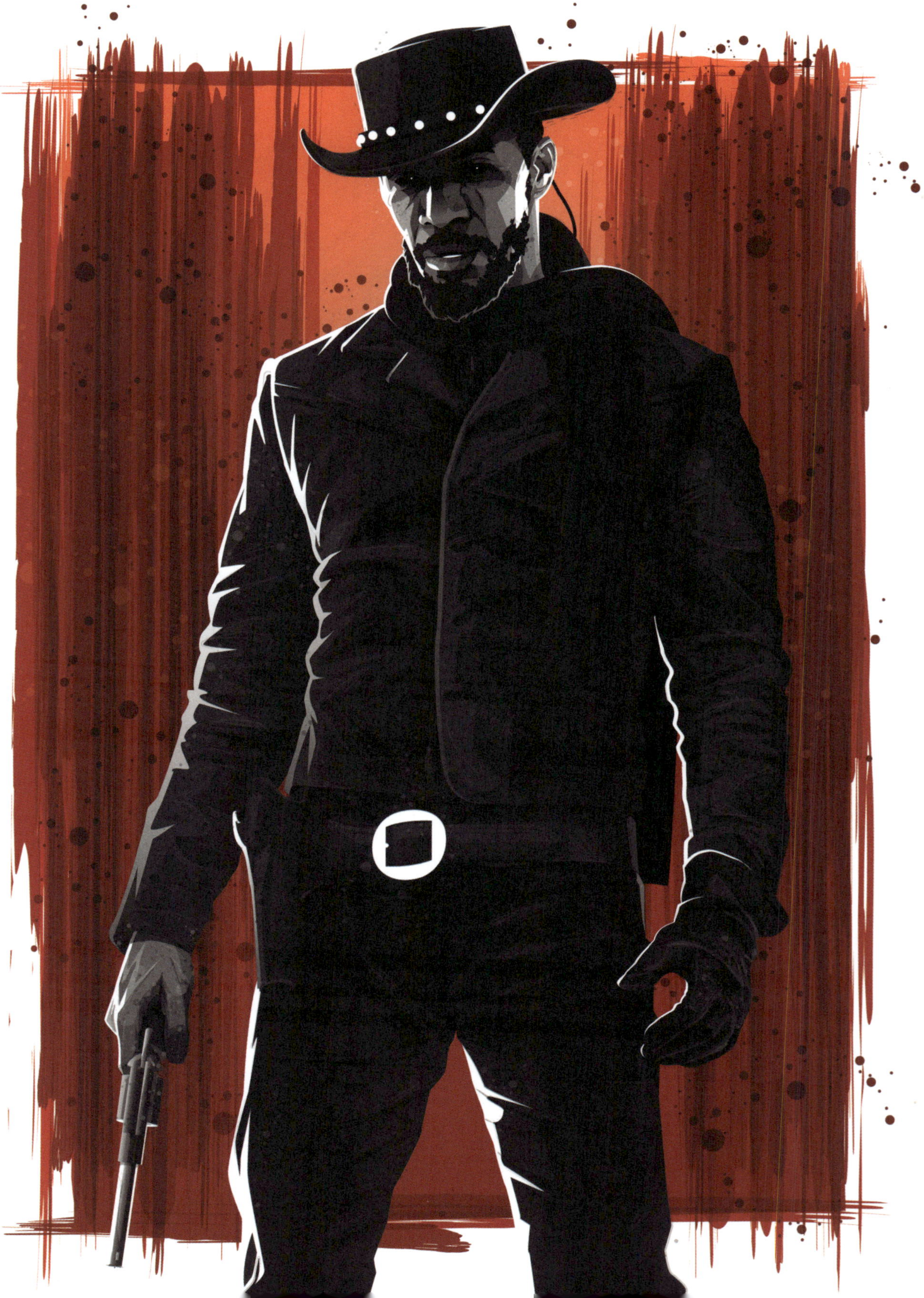

"Django. The D is silent"

"Django.
La D es muda"

- Django -

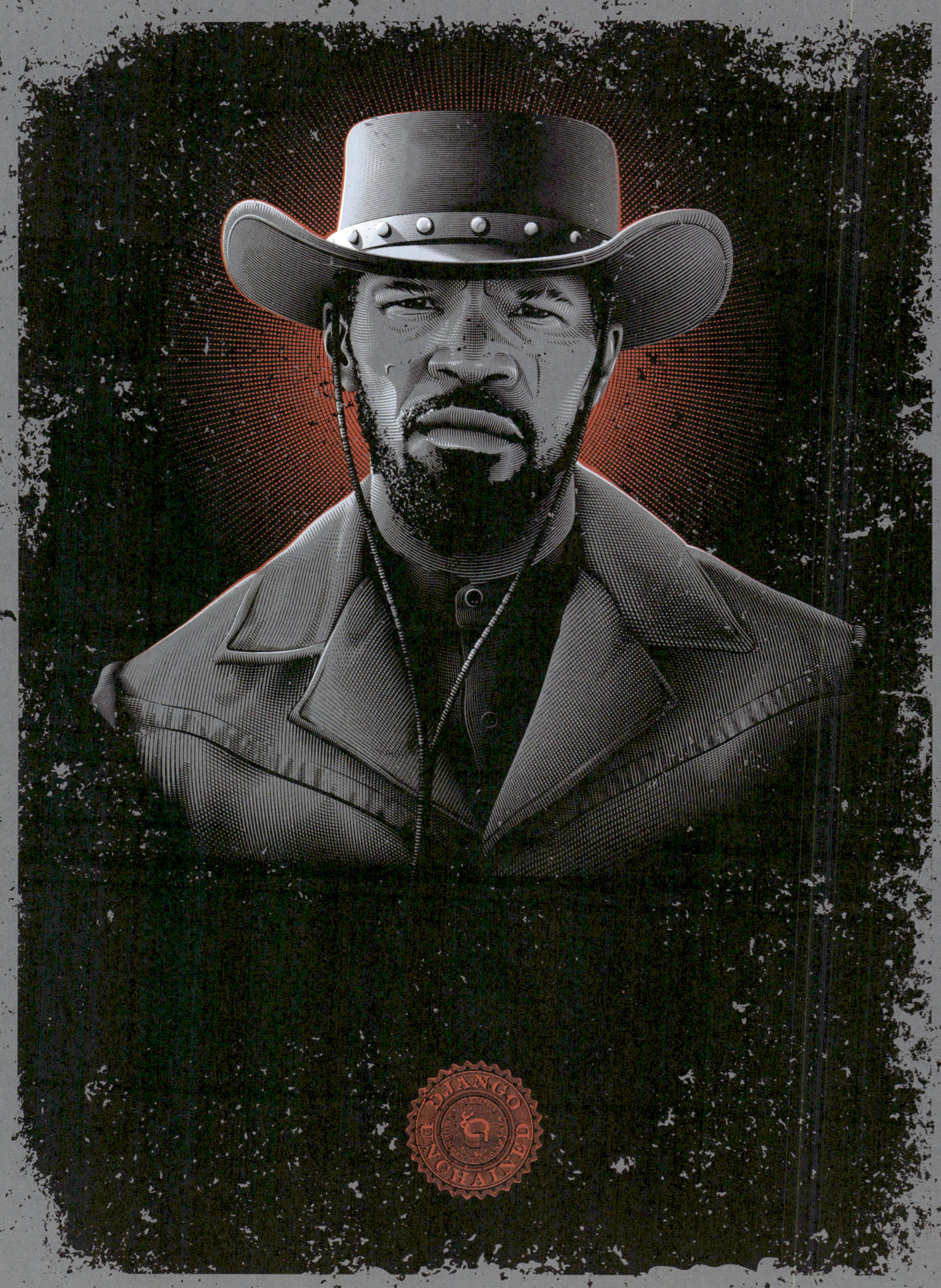
DJANGO
UNCHAINED

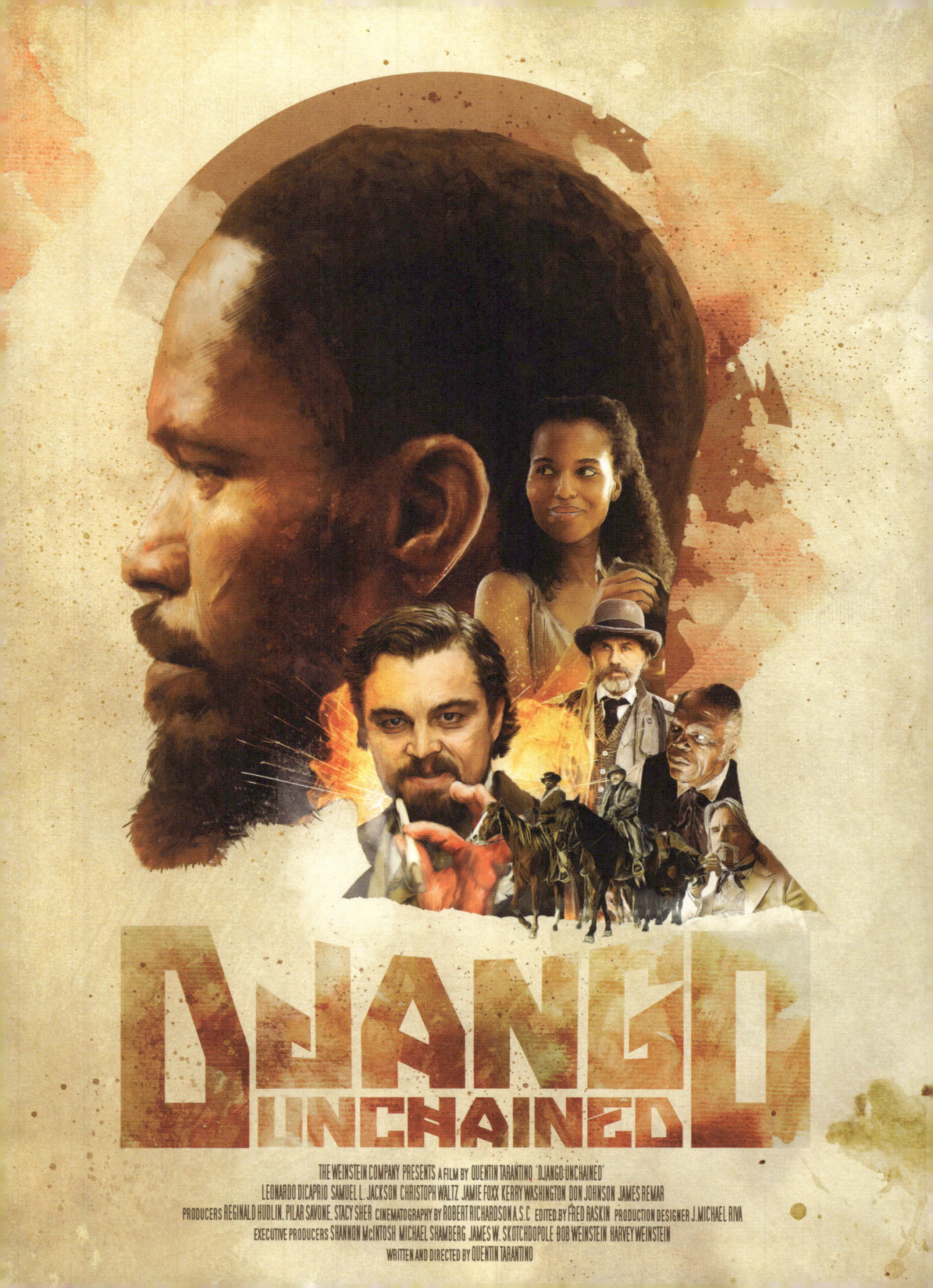
DJANGO
UNCHAINED
THE WEINSTEIN COMPANY PRESENTS A FILM BY QUENTIN TARANTINO "DJANGO UNCHAINED"
LEONARDO DICAPRIO SAMUEL L. JACKSON CHRISTOPH WALTZ JAMIE FOXX KERRY WASHINGTON DON JOHNSON JAMES REMAR
PRODUCERS REGINALD HUDLIN, PILAR SAVONE, STACY SHER CINEMATOGRAPHY BY ROBERT RICHARDSON A.S.C EDITED BY FRED RASKIN PRODUCTION DESIGNER J. MICHAEL RIVA
EXECUTIVE PRODUCERS SHANNON McINTOSH MICHAEL SHAMBERG JAMES W. SKOTCHDOPOLE BOB WEINSTEIN HARVEY WEINSTEIN
WRITTEN AND DIRECTED BY QUENTIN TARANTINO

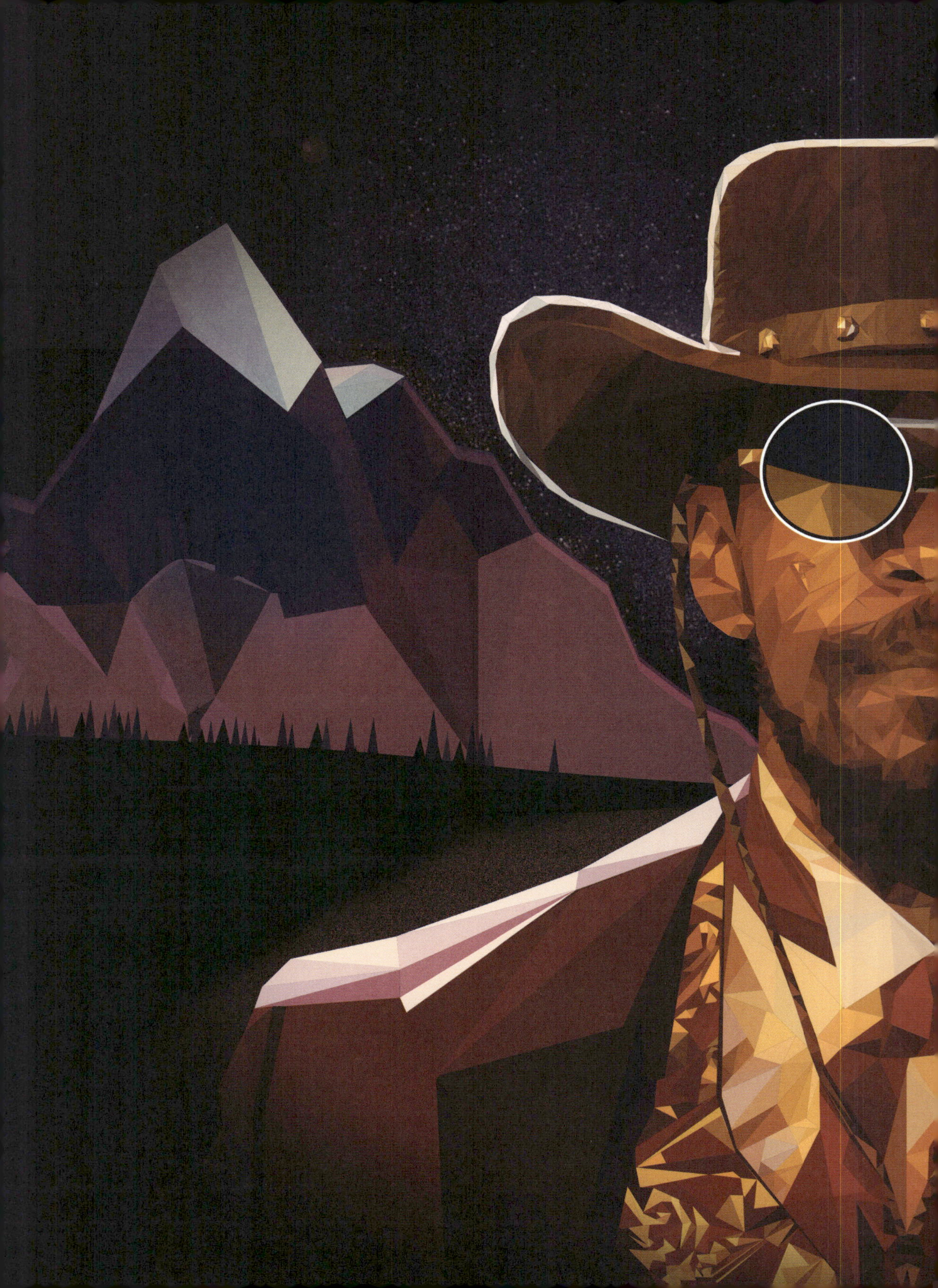

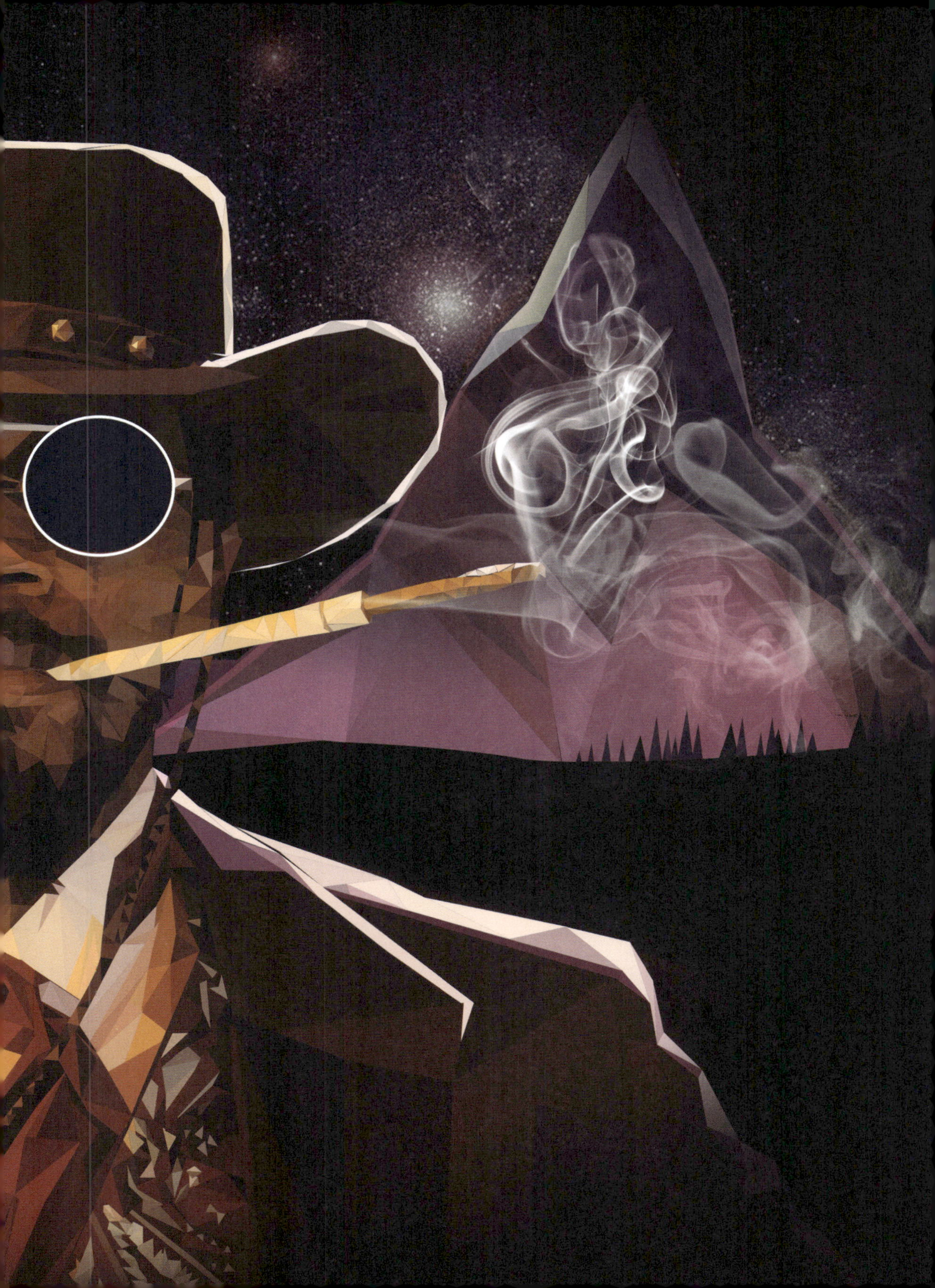

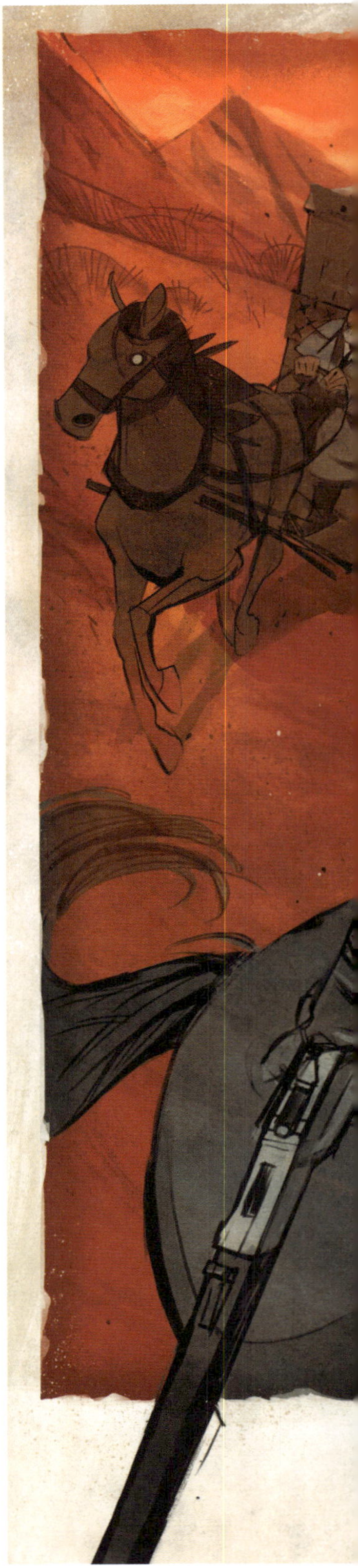

Initially, Quentin Tarantino wrote the part of Django with Will Smith in mind, and in fact the actor was willing to play it. However, he declined at the last moment arguing that "I felt that I only wanted to participate if it was a love story and not a story of revenge. I don't believe in fighting violence with violence...". The role was then offered to Jamie Foxx, who did accept it.

Inicialmente, Quentin Tarantino escribió el papel de Django pensando en Will Smith, y de hecho el actor estaba dispuesto a interpretarlo. Sin embargo declinó en el último momento alegando que "Sentía que la única manera de participar era si se trataba de una historia de amor y no una historia de venganza. No creo en la violencia como reacción a la violencia...". El papel fue entonces ofrecido a Jamie Foxx, quien sí lo aceptó.

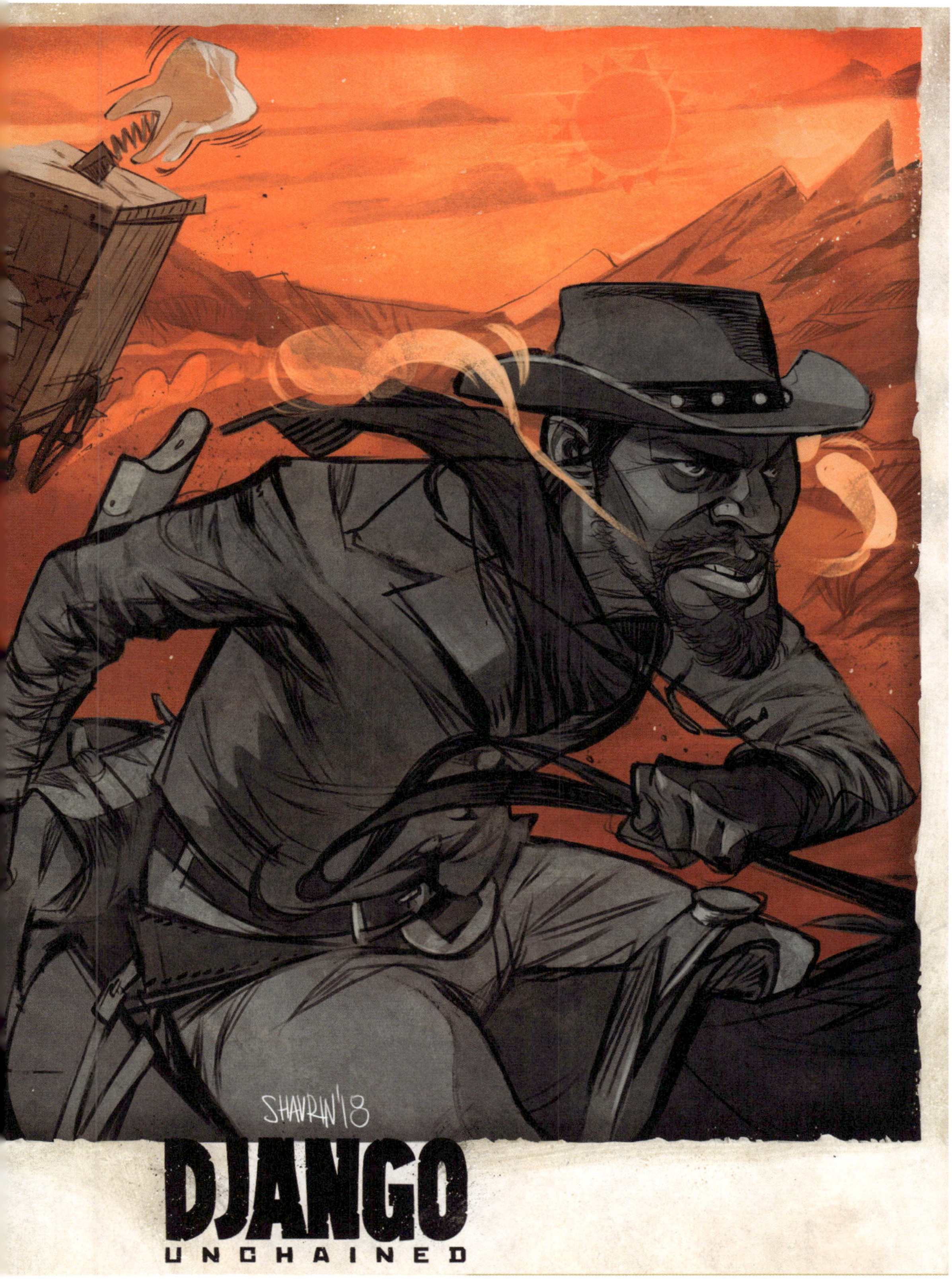
SHAVRIN'18
DJANGO
UNCHAINED

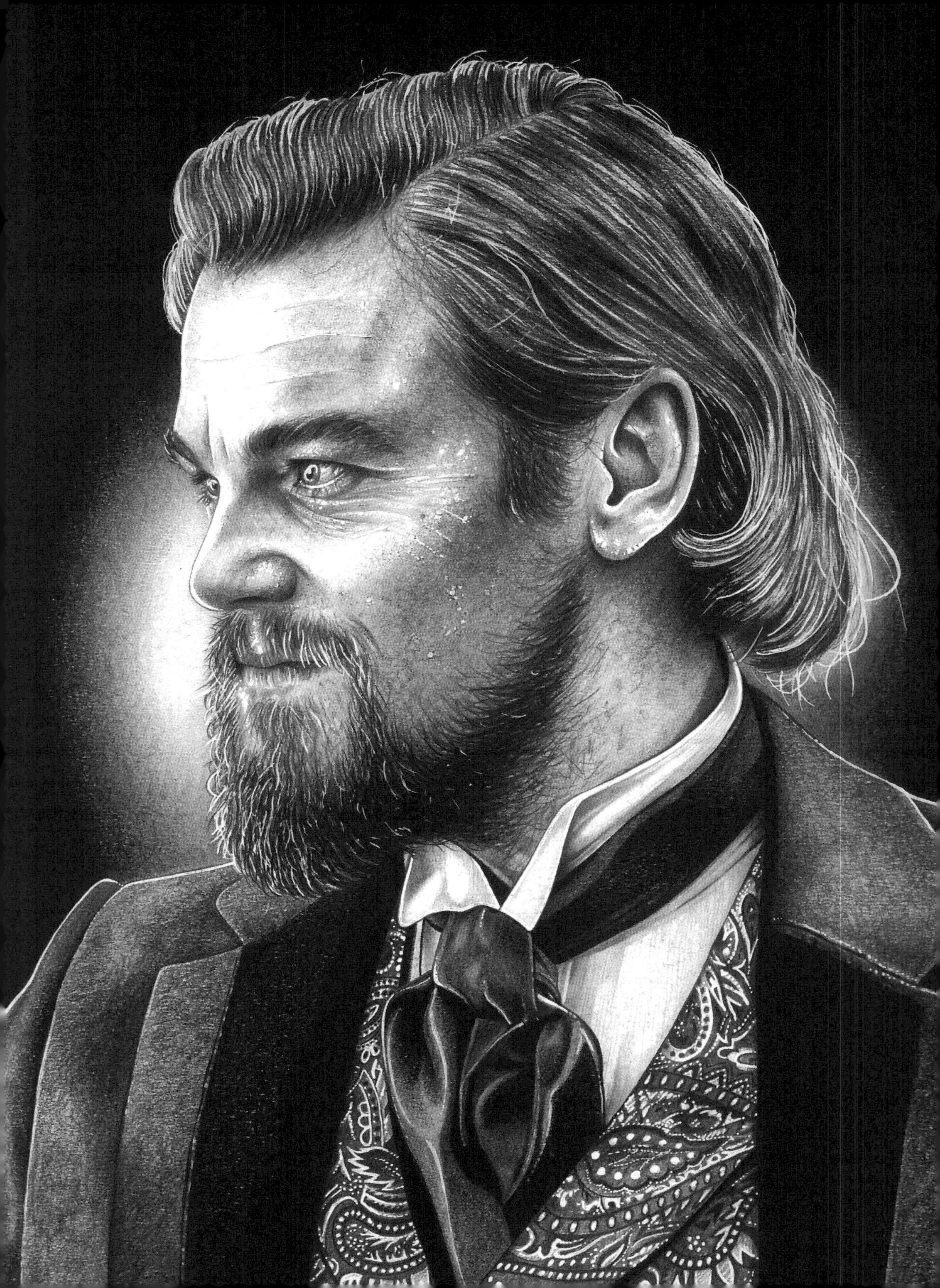

"Gentlemen, you had my curiosity, but now you have my attention"

"Caballeros, ya tenían mi curiosidad, pero ahora tienen mi atención"

- Calvin J. Candie -

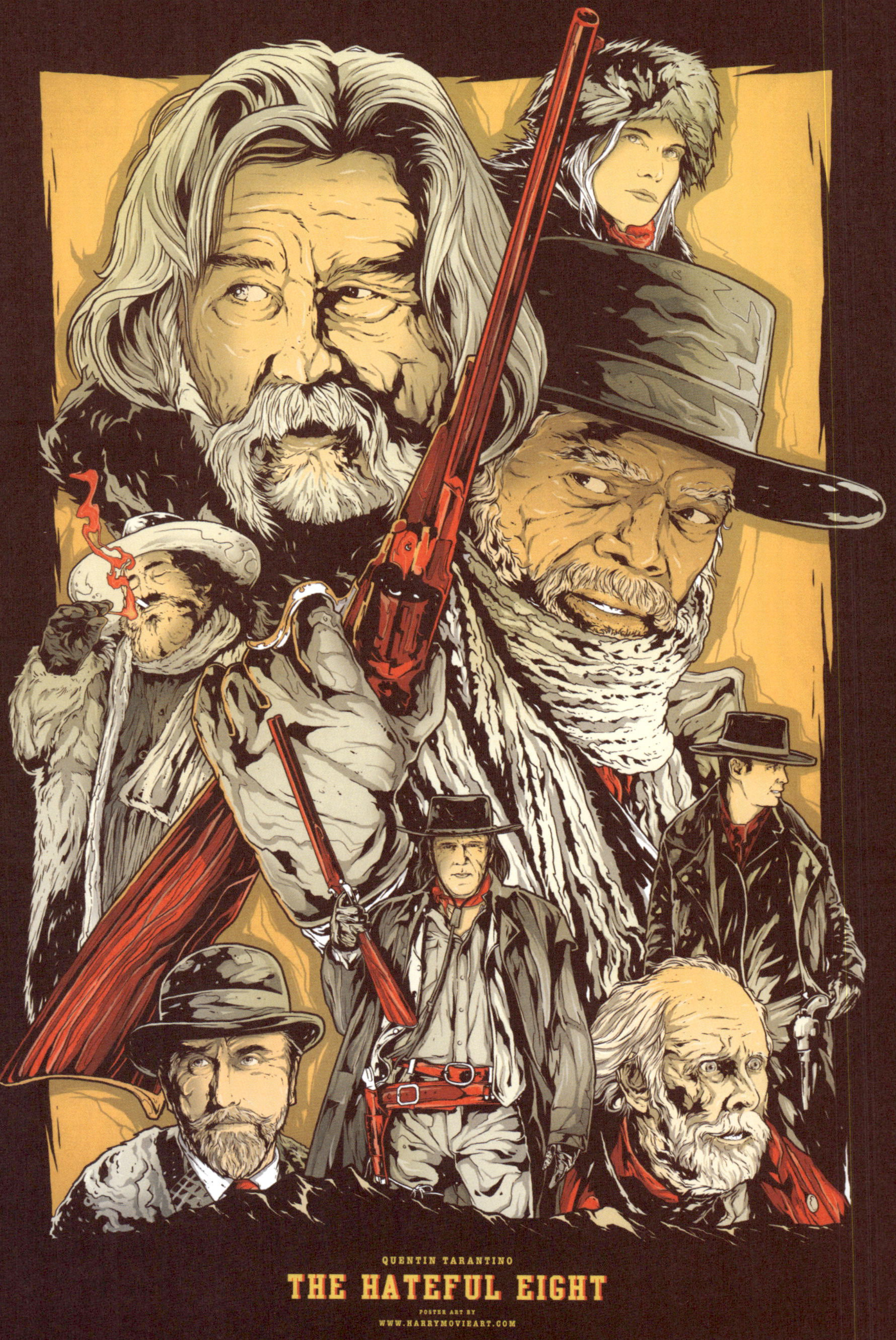
QUENTIN TARANTINO
THE HATEFUL EIGHT
POSTER ART BY
WWW.HARRYMOVIEART.COM

THE HATEFUL EIGHT

2015

In the film, the characters are immersed in the extreme conditions of a heavy snowstorm. The crew and cast shot the film in a 30° refrigerated set.

Tarantino doesn't appear in this film, but his voice does. In chapter 4 of the film (Domergue's Got a Secret), a narrator unexpectedly appears saying word for word what is happening on the screen. It is the director's own particular cameo.

En la película, los personajes se ven inmersos en un escenario extremo debido al fuerte temporal de nieve. Durante el rodaje, el equipo técnico y el reparto filmaron en un set refrigerado de 30 grados.

Tarantino no aparece en este film, pero sí su voz. En el capítulo 4 de la película (Domergue's Got a Secret), y de manera inesperada aparece la figura de un narrador contando literalmente lo que vemos en la pantalla, se trata del cameo particular del propio director.

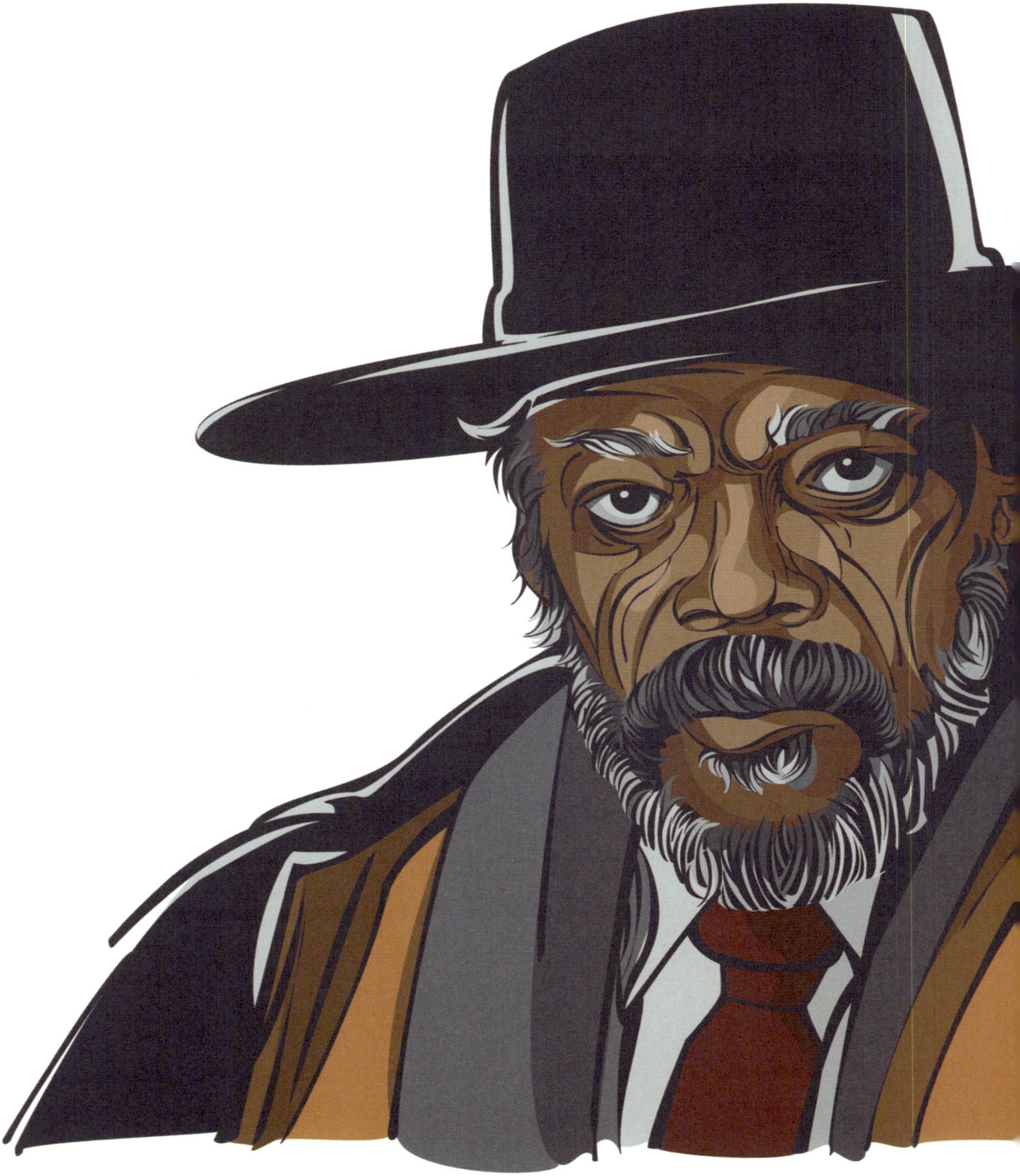

"I don't like taking the Lincoln letter in an'out of the envelope that much"

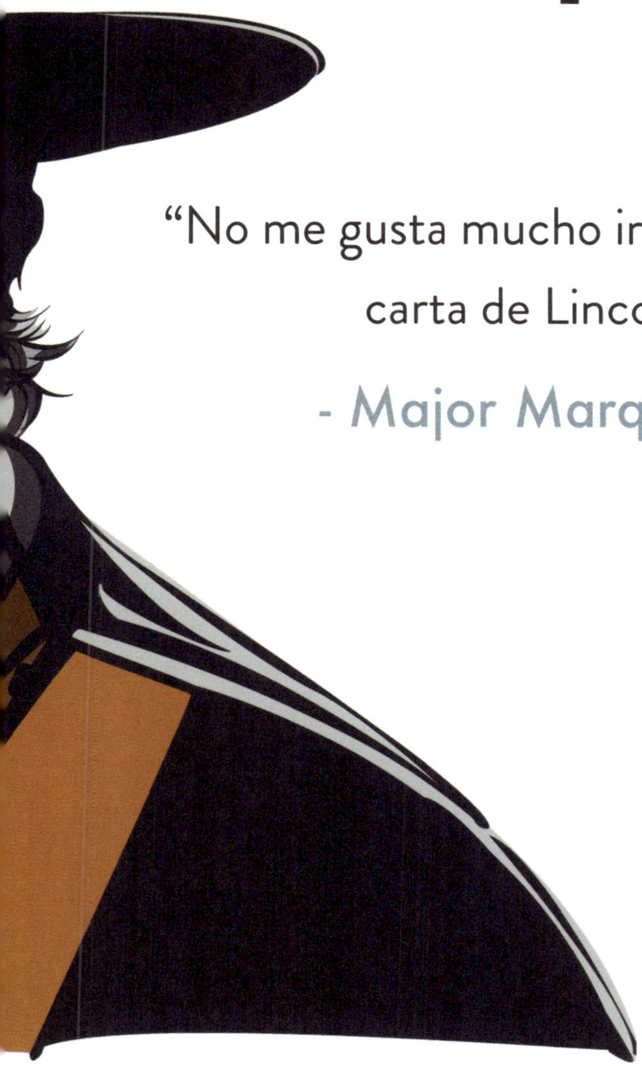

"No me gusta mucho ir metiendo y sacando la carta de Lincoln del sobre"

- Major Marquis Warren -

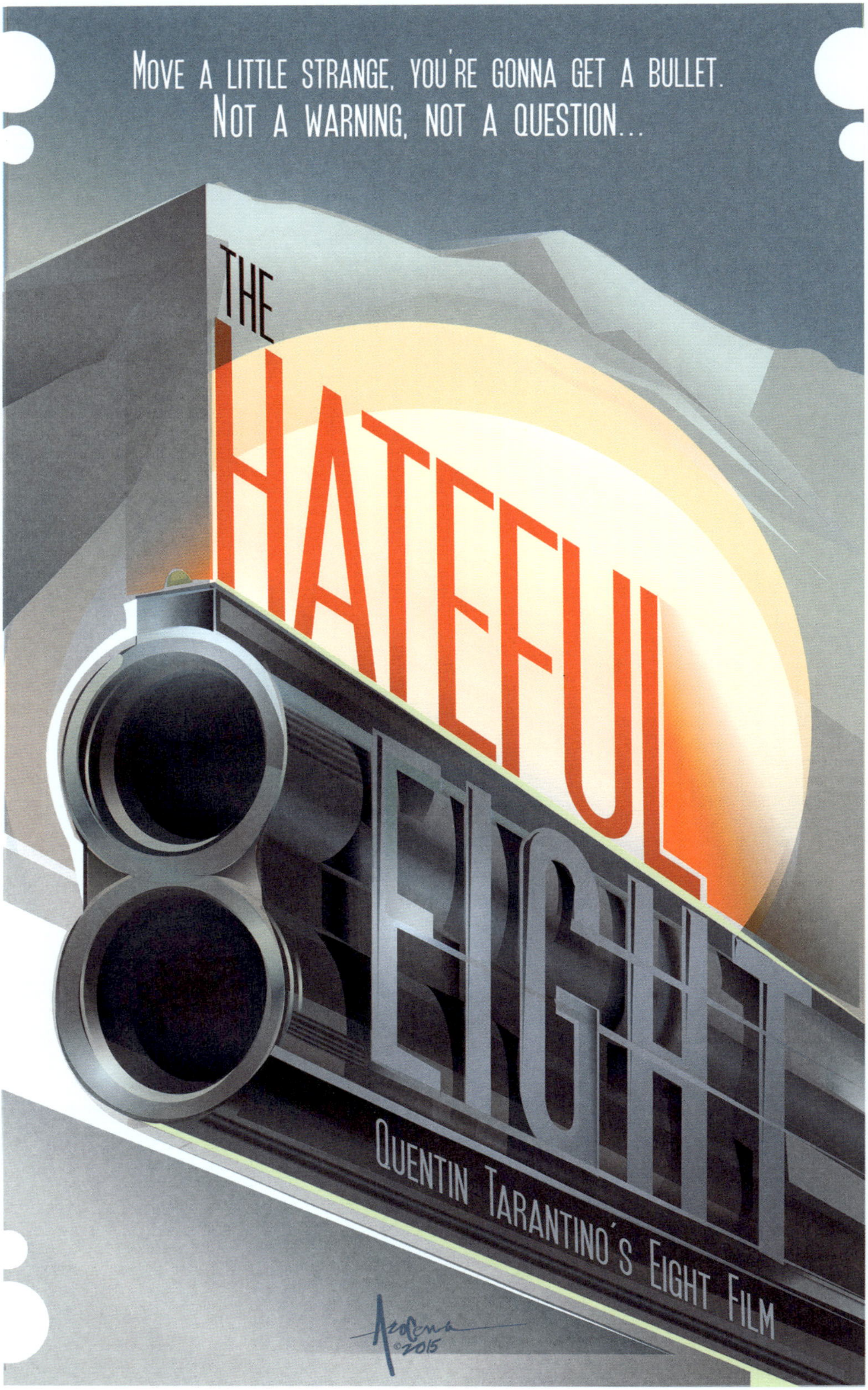
MOVE A LITTLE STRANGE, YOU'RE GONNA GET A BULLET.
NOT A WARNING, NOT A QUESTION...
THE
HATEFUL
EIGHT
QUENTIN TARANTINO'S EIGHT FILM
©2015

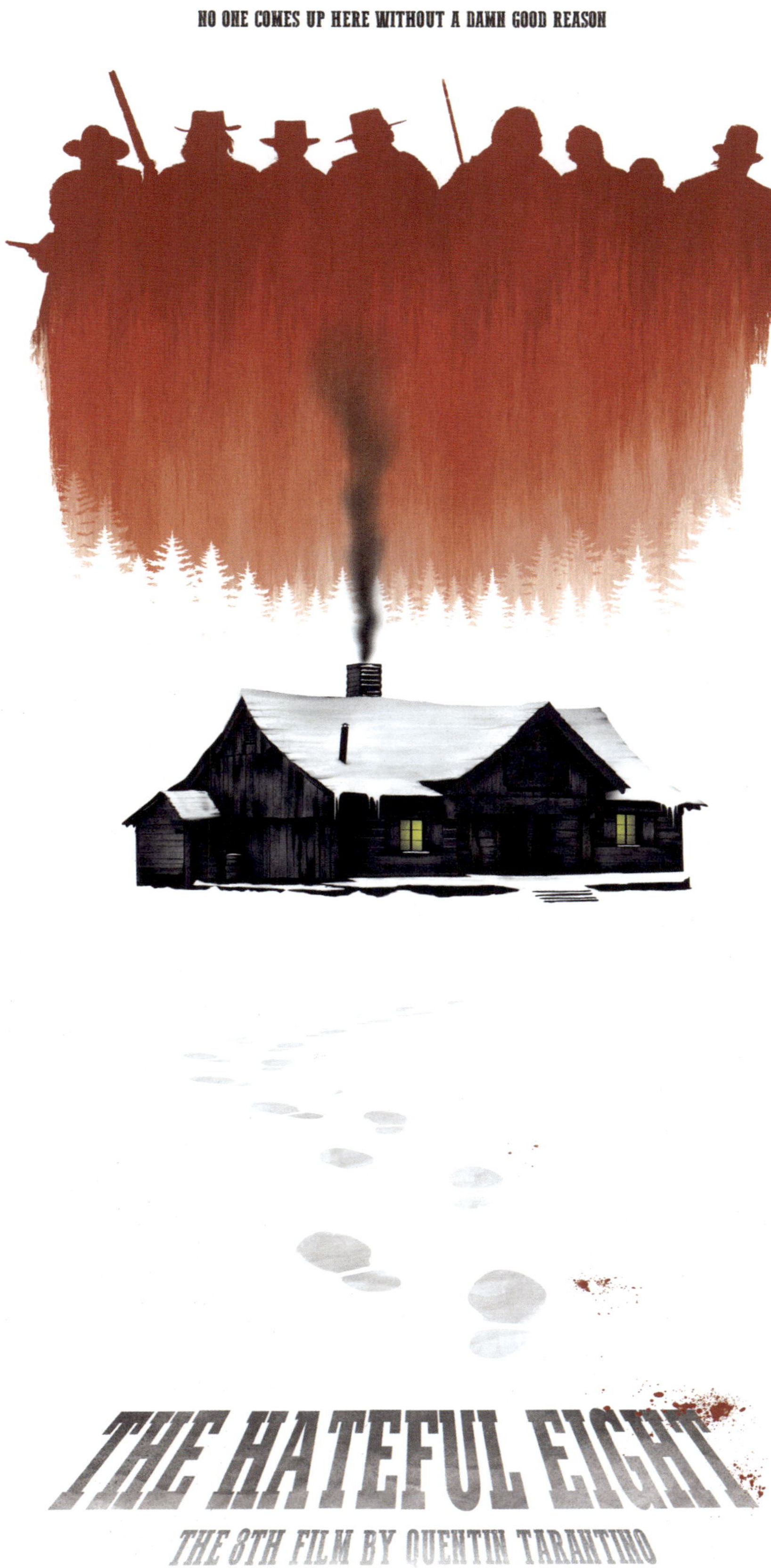
NO ONE COMES UP HERE WITHOUT A DAMN GOOD REASON
THE HATEFUL EIGHT
THE 8TH FILM BY QUENTIN TARANTINO

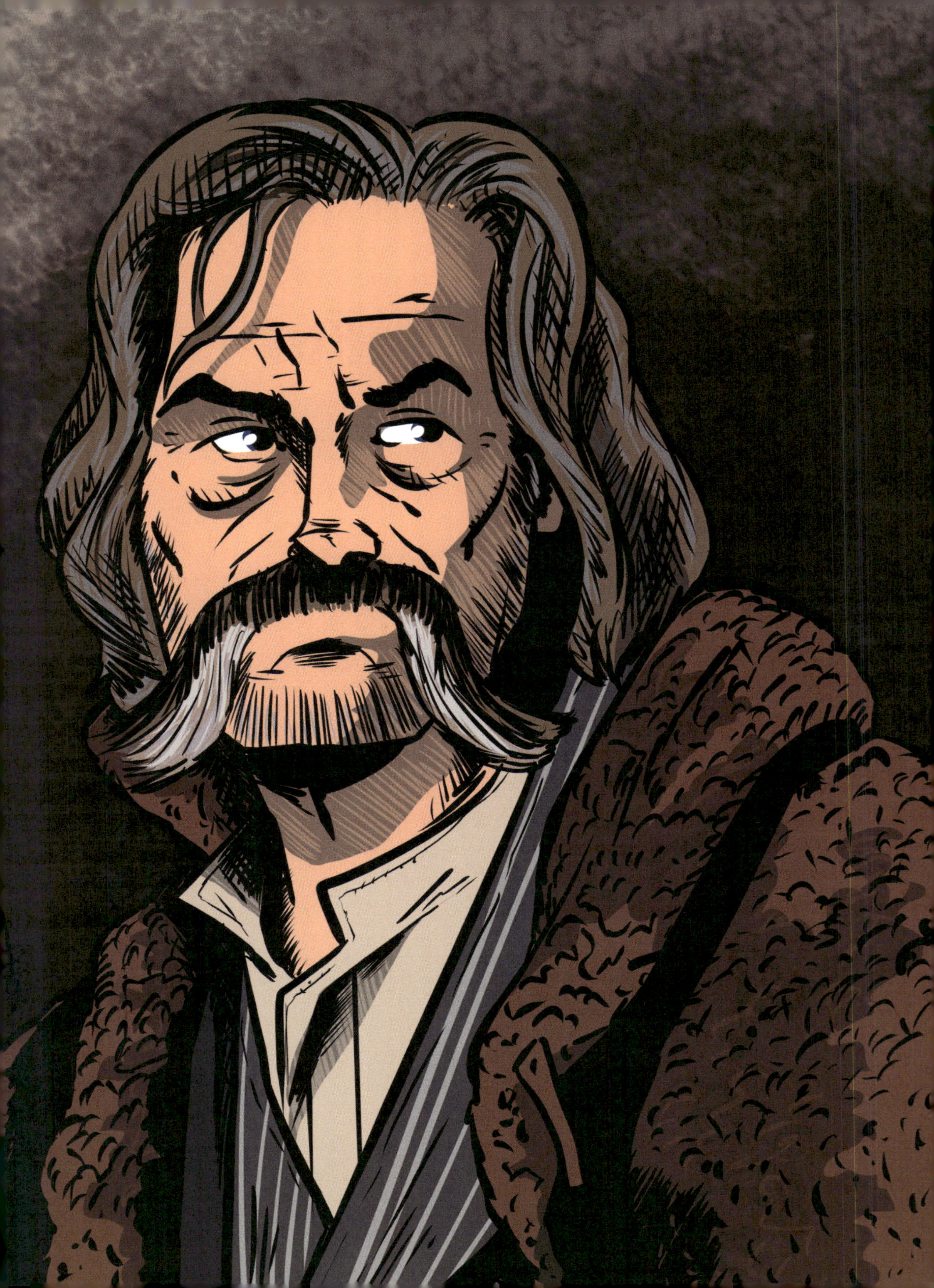

"One of them fellas is not what he says he is..."

"Uno de estos tipos no es quien dice ser..."

- John Ruth -

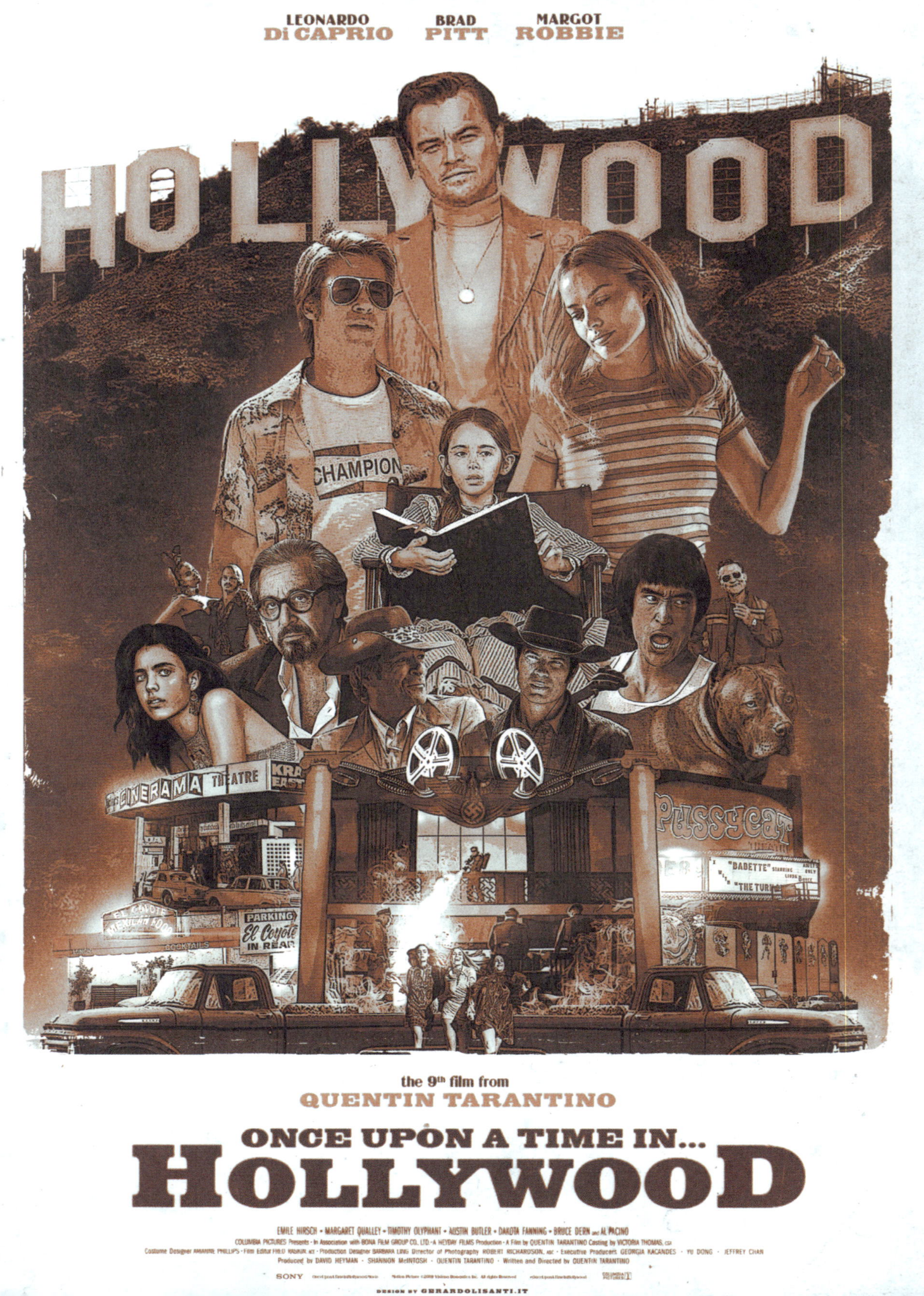
LEONARDO DiCAPRIO
BRAD PITT
MARGOT ROBBIE
HOLLYWOOD
CHAMPION
CINERAMA THEATRE
PUSSYCAT
"DADETTE"
THE TURN
EL COYOTE MEXICAN FOOD
COCKTAILS
PARKING El Coyote IN REAR
the 9th film from
QUENTIN TARANTINO
ONCE UPON A TIME IN...
HOLLYWOOD
EMILE HIRSCH • MARGARET QUALLEY • TIMOTHY OLYPHANT • AUSTIN BUTLER • DAKOTA FANNING • BRUCE DERN and AL PACINO
COLUMBIA PICTURES Presents • In Association with BONA FILM GROUP CO. LTD. • A HEYDAY FILMS Production • A Film by QUENTIN TARANTINO Casting by VICTORIA THOMAS, CSA
Director of Photography ROBERT RICHARDSON, ASC • Executive Producers GEORGIA KACANDES • YU DONG • JEFFREY CHAN
Produced by DAVID HEYMAN • SHANNON McINTOSH • QUENTIN TARANTINO • Written and Directed by QUENTIN TARANTINO
SONY
DESIGN BY GERARDOLISANTI.IT

ONCE UPON A TIME IN HOLLYWOOD

2019

The director's ninth film, set in a tragic moment in American history when Charles Manson and his followers cast a dark shadow over Los Angeles in August 1969, killing seven people, including actress Sharon Tate, Roman Polanski's wife, played by Margot Robbie.

In Once Upon a Time in Hollywood, Tarantino recovers Luke Perry in the role of Wayne Maunder. Perry died on 4 March 2019, having recorded all his scenes.

Novena película del director, y ambientada en un momento trágico de la historia norteamericana en la que Charles Manson y sus seguidores ensombrecieron Los Ángeles en agosto de 1969 asesinando a siete personas incluida la actriz Sharon Tate, esposa de Roman Polanski; y que interpreta Margot Robbie.

En Once Upon a Time in Hollywood, Tarantino recupera a Luke Perry interpretando a Wayne Maunder. Perry murió el 4 de marzo de 2019, habiendo grabado todas sus escenas.

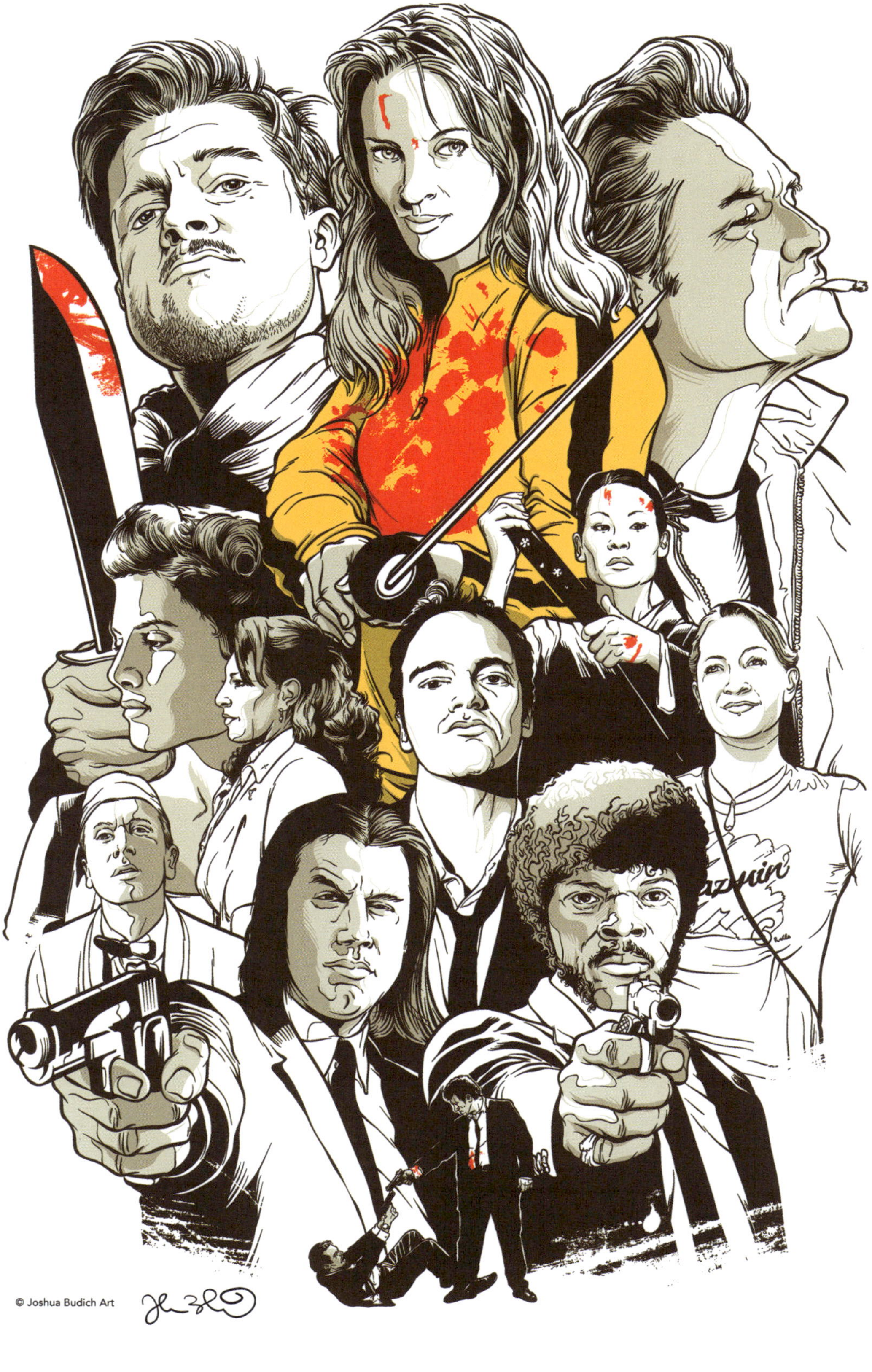

MARK REIHILL

www.markreihill.com
Instagram @mark_reihill
Twitter @markreihill
Facebook Mark Reihill Illustration
© pages 50, 72, 82

Mark lives and works in Ireland and has been a professional illustrator for longer than he cares to remember. He is best known for his work with "the world's best bar", the Dead Rabbit, Grocery & Grog, NYC, illustrating everything from prints and T-shirts to their award winning cocktail menus. He is the artist on several comic books including the award-winning series "Off Girl" and WWII thriller "Ratline".
Mark has worked with Adidas, Jameson, PokerStars, Usborne Publishing and is the (longest running) cover artist for Starburst Magazine with over 70 covers in the cannon. He has also exhibited in official, fully-licensed shows with AMC for the Walking Dead, Fox for American Horror Story and was one of the 50 artists handpicked by CBS to feature in a year-long art exhibition celebrating Star Trek's 50th anniversary. Mark loves Irish whiskey and has an irrational fear of sharks.

Mark vive y trabaja en Irlanda y ha sido ilustrador profesional durante más tiempo del que incluso puede recordar. Se le conoce sobre todo por su trabajo con "the world's best bar", the Dead Rabbit Grocery & Grog en Nueva York, ilustrando de todo, desde estampados y camisetas hasta sus galardonados menús de cócteles. Ha realizado varios comics, incluyendo la premiada serie de "Off Girl" y el thriller de la Segunda Guerra Mundial llamado "Ratline".
Mark ha trabajado con Adidas, Jameson, PokerStars, Usborne Ediciones y es el artista diseñador de las portadas (de más larga duración) para la revista Starburst, con más de 70 portadas.
También ha expuesto en espectáculos oficiales con licencia con la cadena AMC para the Walking Dead, la cadena Fox para American Horror Story y fue uno de los 50 artistas seleccionados por la CBS para participar en una exposición de arte que duró un año entero con motivo del 50 aniversario de Star Trek. A Mark le encanta el whisky irlandés y tiene un miedo irracional a los tiburones.

CRANIODSGN

www.craniodsgn.es
Instagram @craniodsgn
Behance behance.net/craniodsgn
Twitter @craniodsgn
Dribbble: dribbble.com/craniodsgn
© pages 18-19, 46-47, 52, 60, 64

Alejandro García is a vector illustrator and graphic designer from Valencia, working under the pseudonym CranioDsgn since 2006.
The main sources of inspiration for this vector craftsman are science fiction and suspense films. The works of Tarantino, Nolan, Kubric, Coppola, J. J. Abrams, Darren Onorofsky and Hitchcock serve as the basis for the creation of personal projects such as alternative posters for films and series.
His great music fetishes are Post-Rock instrumental music and Punk Rock-Hardcore. Extremely meticulous, he achieves his detailed style by scrutinising graphic novels by Alan Moore, Frank Miller, Neil Adams and Jim Lee, with groups such as Mono, Russian Circles, Lagwagon, No use For a Name or Queen playing at full volume in his studio. Design, colour and fun from Kozik, Jason Freeny, Kaws and Ron English accompany him when he is immersed in his most artistic facet, customising and even creating some of these pieces. CranioDsgn works as a freelance for advertising agencies, design studios, magazines and fashion brands. In addition, whenever possible, he participates in collective exhibitions and projects in different art galleries around the world.

Alejandro García es un ilustrador vectorial y diseñador gráfico nacido en Valencia, que trabaja bajo el pseudónimo de CranioDsgn desde el año 2006.
Este artesano del vector tiene como principales fuentes de inspiración los campos del cine de ciencia ficción y suspense. Las obras de Tarantino, Nolan, Kubric, Coppola, J.J.Abrams, Darren Onorofsky y Hitchcock, sirven como base para la creación de proyectos personales como carteles alternativos de películas y series.
Sus grandes fetiches sonoros son la música Post-Rock Instrumental y el Punk Rock-Hardcore. Extremadamente meticuloso, consigue su estilo detallista analizando con lupa novelas gráficas de Alan Moore, Frank Miller, Neil Adams y Jim Lee, mientras grupos como Mono, Russian Circles, Lagwagon, No use For a Name o Queen resuenan bastante alto en su estudio. Diseño, color y diversión de la mano de Kozik, Jason Freeny, Kaws, Ron English. Le acompañan cuando desarrolla su faceta más plástica, customizando e incluso creando, alguna de estas piezas. CranioDsgn trabaja como freelance para agencias de publicidad, estudios de diseño, revistas y marcas de moda. Además, siempre que puede, participa en exposiciones y proyectos colectivos en diferentes galerías de arte de todo el mundo.

ILYA KUVSHINOV

www.patreon.com/Kuvshinov_Ilya
Instagram: @kuvshinov_ilya
© pages 58

Ilya Kuvshinov is a Russian illustrator with a significant social media following; on Instagram, Twitter and DeviantArt. On Instagram alone, 1,6M followers from all over the world eagerly await his latest posts!

Ilya Kuvshinov es un ilustrador ruso con un importante seguimiento en las redes sociales; en Instagram, Twitter y DeviantArt. Sólo en Instagram, 1,6 millones de seguidores de todo el mundo esperan ansiosamente su próxima publicación.

RICHARD DAVIES

www.turksworks.co.uk
Instagram @turksworks
Twitter @turksworks
Facebook @turksworksillustration
© pages 85

Based in beautiful Carmarthenshire, Wales, Richard has worked as a graphic designer and illustrator for almost fifteen years. Inspired by the movie poster and commercial art of his youth, Richard's work is predominantly used in the entertainment and publishing industries.
Over the last few years Richard has gradually built up an impressive client base, from large film studios such as Disney and Twentieth Century Fox to world renowned publishers such as Rolling Stone Magazine and Random House. His commercial work has also led him to exhibit in various galleries in Los Angeles, New York, Marseille, Vienna and Zurich as well as published in various design and pop culture publications throughout the world.

Afincado en la hermosa Carmarthenshire, Gales, Richard ha trabajado como diseñador gráfico e ilustrador durante casi quince años. Inspirado por los pósters de películas y el arte comercial en su juventud, el trabajo de Richard se utiliza predominantemente en las industrias del entretenimiento y en el sector editorial.
En los últimos años, Richard ha ido acumulando una impresionante cartera de clientes, desde grandes estudios de cine como Disney y Twentieth Century Fox hasta editores de renombre mundial como la revista Rolling Stone y el grupo editorial Random House. Su trabajo comercial también lo ha llevado a exhibir en varias galerías de Los Ángeles, Nueva York, Marsella, Viena y Zúrich, así como a publicar en diversas publicaciones de diseño y cultura pop en todo el mundo.

JOSHUA BUDICH

www.joshuabudich.com
Instagram @jbudich
Twitter @jbudich
Facebook @jbudich
© pages 12, 26, 30-31, 32, 48, 68, 102

Joshua Budich is an independent illustrator working for numerous galleries, including Gallery 1988 and Spoke Art movie studios, and media outlets around the globe. Inspired by a love for the pop culture of his youth, his primary focus is on screenprints that celebrate popular movies, animated shows and more. Budich graduated from the University of Maryland Baltimore County with a Bachelor of Fine Arts (Imaging and Digital Arts) in 2000. He enjoys cooking with his wife, drawing with his son, and reading to his daughter. He lives in the Baltimore/District of Columbia area with his wife and their two children.

Joshua Budich es un ilustrador independiente que trabaja para numerosas galerías, incluida la Gallery 1988 y los estudios de cine Spoke Art, así como medios informativos de todo el mundo. Inspirado por el amor a la cultura pop de su juventud, se centra principalmente en la serigrafía sobre películas populares, espectáculos animados y mucho más. Budich se graduó en la Universidad de Maryland (Condado de Baltimore) con una Licenciatura en Bellas Artes (Ilustración y Artes Digitales) en 2000. Le gusta cocinar con su esposa, dibujar con su hijo y leerle a su hija. Vive en el área de Baltimore/Distrito de Columbia con su esposa y sus dos hijos.

STANLEY CHOW

www.stanleychow.co.uk
Instagram @stan_chow
Twitter @stan_chow
Facebook @stanchowillustration
© pages 22, 38

Stanley Chow is an illustrator from Manchester. He has been freelancing for nearly 25 years. Stanley specialises in illustrating faces. His clients include The New Yorker, The New York Times, Time, Manchester United, HBO, Netflix and Twitter.

Stanley Chow es un ilustrador de Manchester. Lleva casi 25 años trabajando de forma autónoma. Stanley está especializado en ilustrar rostros. Entre sus clientes se encuentran The New Yorker, The New York Times, Time, Manchester United, HBO, Netflix y Twitter.

CHOD ARTIST

www. chodartist.com
Instagram @chodartist
Facebook @chodartist
© pages 33

Chod's earliest recollection of being affected by art was by a book of Grimm's Fairy Tales Illustrated by Benvenuti. At three years old he would ask for "The Old Woman of the Mountains" to be read over and over. In the story there was an illustration of a girl's skin draped over a branch of a tree. He remembers staring at it and noticing that it was so different from every other picture in all of his other books. Since that point Chod has always been drawn to the bit off. He tries to make sure that whatever he produces is something that the three year old in him would want to look at over and over again.

El primer recuerdo de la influencia del arte para Chod fue a través de un libro de cuentos de los hermanos Grimm, ilustrado por Benvenuti. A los 3 años, pedía que le leyeran una y otra vez el libro "The Old Woman of the Mountains". En el libro, había una ilustración de la piel de una niña envolviendo la rama de un árbol. Recuerda mirarlo fijamente y darse cuenta de que era realmente diferente de las demás imágenes en todos sus otros libros. Desde ese momento, Chod siempre se ha sentido atraído por aquello que está fuera de lo común. Intenta asegurarse de que cualquier cosa que produce es algo que a aquel niño de 3 años que lleva en su interior le gustaría mirar una y otra vez.

TRACIE CHING

www.tracieching.com
Instagram @tracieching
Twitter @tracieching
Facebook @traciechingdesign
© pages 54, 57, 76, 84

Living and working in Washington, DC, Tracie Ching is a self-taught digital artist specializing in complex, graphic portraiture. Her work often involves a limited palette – a tendency-turned-style after years of working in the medium of silkscreen prints.
While commissioned for a wide range of projects including commercial athletic apparel, editorial illustration, and gallery work, Tracie Ching is best known for her alternative movie posters.

Viviendo y trabajando en Washington DC, Tracie Ching es una artista digital autodidacta especializada en retratos gráficos complejos. Su trabajo a menudo implica una paleta limitada; una tendencia convertida en estilo después de años trabajando en el medio de la serigrafía.
A la vez que se encarga de una amplia gama de proyectos, incluidos la ropa deportiva comercial, la ilustración editorial y el trabajo en galerías, Tracie Ching es más conocida por sus carteles de películas alternativas.

BOB RISSETTO

www.bobrissetto.com
www.linkedin.com/in/bobrissetto
© pages 63

Bob has been a 2D artist working out of Chicago for many years. His sense of color and flat design lends itself well to animation which is one of his biggest passions. Mix in a nostalgic love of toys, video games, and movies, and it's no wonder why he rarely goes outside. Some might call him a "professional nerd" but to him it's all art! You can find him watching cartoons with a big bowl of cereal on Saturday mornings.

Bob ha sido un artista del 2D que ha trabajado en Chicago durante muchos años. Su sentido del color y del diseño plano se prestan bien a la animación, que es una de sus mayores pasiones. Está inmerso en un amor nostálgico por los juguetes, los videojuegos y las películas, y no es de extrañar que rara vez salga a la calle. Puede que algunos lo llamen "cerebrito profesional", pero, para él, ¡todo es arte! Se le puede encontrar viendo dibujos animados con un gran tazón de cereales los sábados por la mañana.

REHA SAKAR

www.rehasakar.com
Instagram @_wardancer
Facebook @reha.skr
© pages 70

Reha Sakar is living in Vancouver Canada, working in gaming/movie industry, and also doing watercolor paintings. Born in Istanbul, since kid he has been painting with his mother, who is also an artist. They used to spend hours painting. She then pushed him to take some courses on 3D and Photoshop in 2002. Since then, he has been working on Television, doing stuff for games and movies.

Reha Sakar vive en Vancouver, Canadá, trabajando en la industria de los videojuegos y el cine. También hace pinturas con acuarela. Nacido en Estambul, desde niño comenzó pintando con su madre, que también es artista. Solían pasar horas pintando, hasta que ella le animó a hacer algunos cursos de 3D y Photoshop en 2002. Desde entonces, ha estado trabajando en televisión, realizando encargos para juegos y películas.

MAYNOON WU

www.behance.net/maynoonwu
Instagram @skyseed_
Facebook @SkyseedIllustrations
© pages 74-75

Maynoon Wu is a South African based artist who graduated with Honours from the University of Witwatersrand in Johannesburg, South Africa with a Bachelor's degree in Fine Art in 2017. She is a self-taught digital artist.
From a very young age, she has enjoyed creating works and furthering her skills in art which is what had led to her decision of studying it as her major in university. Her passion is in digital art and illustration but she also enjoys experimentation with different mediums, particularly that of sculpture. The current interest in her work is how pop culture influences us and the ways that we look at icons and how they have an impact on us.

Maynoon Wu es una artista sudafricana graduada en la Universidad de Witwatersrand en Johannesburgo, Sudáfrica, con una licenciatura en Bellas Artes en 2017. Es una artista digital autodidacta.
Desde muy joven, ha disfrutado creando obras y mejorando sus habilidades en el arte, así tomó la decisión de estudiarlo como su especialidad en la universidad. Su pasión es el arte digital y la ilustración, pero también disfruta de la experimentación con diferentes medios, particularmente el de la escultura. El interés actual en su trabajo se centra en la cultura pop, cómo nos influye, y cómo los iconos pueden llegar a impactarnos.

GEDO GFX

Instagram @gedogfx
© pages 40-41, 110-111

Gedo is based in Egypt working as a freelancer, he defines himself as a "Digital artist" and is a painting, film and art in general lover.

Gedo trabaja como freelance desde Egipto, se define a sí mismo como un "artista digital" y es un amante de la pintura, el cine y el arte en general.

BEN BRUNSDEN

www.benedictbrunsden.com
Instagram @benedictbrunsden
© pages 86-87

Benedict is a Creative Motion and Illustration designer based in Leeds, England where he currently works for Dynamic as a Design and Media Manager.
His passion for Tarantino can be recognised by his large collection of Vinyl Soundtracks and his outstanding artwork. See his website for more details.

Benedict es un diseñador creativo de ilustración y movimiento con sede en Leeds, Inglaterra, donde actualmente trabaja para Dynamic como Design and Media Manager.
Su pasión por Tarantino puede ser reconocida por su gran colección de bandas sonoras en vinilo y sus excepcionales obras de arte que pueden ser vistas en su página web.

HARDIAN

www.behance.net/hardianjp
Instagram @hardianjp
© pages 94-95

Born in Surabaya, Indonesia in 1997. He is currently studying Creative Media & Game Technologies at Saxion University of Applied Sciences. Previously, he has studied Visual Communication Design at Petra Christian University in his hometown Surabaya.
As a designer, he focused himself working in the field of Graphic Design. In his journey, he discovered what was called a vector illustration and fell in love with it since he first found it.
This world has many great vector illustrators, and he thrives on to be one of them someday in the future. The thing he likes when making art or design work is that he is always able to learn new things and lessons every day.

Nació en Surabaya, Indonesia, en 1997. Actualmente estudia comunicación audiovisual y tecnología en la Universidad de Ciencias Aplicadas de Saxion. Anteriormente, ha estudiado diseño en la Petra Christian University en su ciudad natal de Surabaya.
Como diseñador, se centró en el campo del diseño gráfico. En esa etapa, descubrió lo que se llamó ilustración vectorial y se enamoró de ella.
En un mundo con tan grandes ilustradores vectoriales, él prospera para ser uno de ellos algún día en el futuro. Lo que más le gusta del arte y el diseño, es que siempre puede aprender cosas y lecciones nuevas todos los días.

BENEDICT WOODHEAD

www.benedictwoodhead.com
Instagram @benedict_woodhead
Twitter @WoodheadArt
Facebook @benedictwoodhead
© pages 67, 97

Benedict is a graphic artist based in York, UK. His work has been exhibited in Galleries from LA to Barcelona. He has produced work for Lionsgate, the Poster Posse and regularly exhibits with Hero Complex Gallery in LA.
Today, his obsession and passion is to produce work which re-designs images from popular culture using digital media. Once Benedict has conceived and developed an idea, he aims to create a brand-new composition which sums up an entire concept in one complete design.

Benedict es un artista gráfico con sede en York, Reino Unido. Su obra ha sido expuesta en galerías de todo el mundo, desde Los Ángeles a Barcelona. Ha producido trabajos para Lionsgate, Poster Posse y expone regularmente en Hero Complex Gallery en Los Ángeles.
Hoy, su obsesión y pasión es producir un trabajo que rediseña imágenes de la cultura popular utilizando medios digitales. Una vez que ha concebido y desarrollado una idea, Benedict trata de crear una composición que resuma un concepto nuevo en un diseño completo.

RUBEN IRELAND

www.rubenireland.com
Instagram @rubenireland
Facebook @rubenirelandillustration
© pages 36

Using a carefully cultivated mixed media digital process, Ruben creates Stoic, minimalist portraits of strong characters. Often female, adorned with flowers and animal features, they act as totems for loss and solitude but also inner strength, resilience and quiet focused power. Although often more drawn towards inward facing themes, Ruben's work sometimes also looks at popular culture, capturing movie scenes and well known characters, inspired by the films of Quentin Tarantino and Luc Besson.

Utilizando un cuidadoso proceso digital de medios mixtos, Ruben crea retratos estoicistas y minimalistas de personajes con caracter. A menudo femeninas, adornadas con flores y rasgos animales, actúan como tótems de la soledad, pero también como fuerza interior, resistencia y poder. Aunque a menudo se siente más atraído hacia los temas internos, el trabajo de Ruben a veces también aborda la cultura popular, capturando escenas de películas y personajes conocidos, inspirados en las películas de Quentin Tarantino y Luc Besson.

JEREMY SCOTT

jscottart3.wixsite.com/jeremyscottart
Instagram @jeremyscottart
© pages 16-17, 28

Jeremy was born and raised in a small mining town in the northern forrest of Manitoba, Canada. After highschool he studied animation before continuing his education at Brandon University where he received a bachelor's degree in Fine Art.
For as long as he can remember Jeremy has been obsessed with all things pop culture. Today, at 37, his love of television, movies, and comic books continue to inform his work and the naming of his pets.
Jeremy Scott is a painter and illustrator living in Winnipeg, Manitoba with his wife, Jen, and their dog, Ripley.

Jeremy nació y se crió en un pequeño pueblo minero en el norte de Manitoba, Canadá. Después de la secundaria, estudió animación antes de continuar su educación en la Universidad de Brandon, donde se graduó en Bellas Artes.
Desde que recuerda, Jeremy ha estado obsesionado con la cultura pop. Hoy, a los 37 años, su amor por la televisión, el cine y los cómics continúa alimentando su trabajo.
Actualmente, Jeremy Scott es un pintor e ilustrador que vive en Winnipeg, Manitoba con su esposa, Jen, y su perro, Ripley.

ANKA ECKES

www.artstation.com/wron
© pages 15

Anna Eckes is an architect and concept artist, currently based in Cracow. Her personal work is focused on the relationship of architecture and digital technologies and the erosion of borders between materiality and virtuality in our contemporary environment. When she's not designing video games or architecture in some remote corner of the world, you can probably spot her painting while rewatching Reservoir Dogs.

Anna Eckes es una arquitecta y artista conceptual, actualmente viviendo en Cracovia. Su trabajo personal se centra en la relación entre la arquitectura y las tecnologías digitales, y la erosión de las fronteras entre la materialidad y la virtualidad en nuestro entorno contemporáneo. Cuando no está diseñando videojuegos o arquitectura en algún rincón remoto del mundo, es probable que puedas encontrarla pintando mientras vuelve a ver Reservoir Dogs.

ŻANETA ANTOSIK

www.behance.net/zanetaantosik
Instagram @zanetaantosik
Facebook @AntosikZaneta
© pages 7

Żaneta Antosik lives and creates in Poland as a freelance.
In her colorful works - mainly portraits, she combines drawing with digital techniques & textures.

Żaneta Antosik vive y desarrolla su actividad como freelance en Polonia . En sus coloridos trabajos, principalmente retratos, combina el dibujo con técnicas y texturas digitales.

JAMES OCONNELL

www.james-oconnell.com
Instagram @jamesp0p
Dribbble dribbble.com/jamesp0p
© pages 34, 53

James Oconnell is a Manchester based creative who has a passion for mixing colour and lines.
He applies his minimalistic style to a variety of themes and has created work for the likes of Riot Games, Wired Magazine, Youtube, BBC and The Atlantic to name a few. He is hugely inspired by contemporary pop culture in all its forms - from motion pictures, music to advertising and sport.
Simplicity is the key to his work where he strives to reduce the level of detail to allow the expression of the idea to reign supreme.

James Oconnell es un creativo afincado en Manchester con una fuerte pasión por mezclar colores y líneas. Aplica su estilo minimalista a una variedad de temas, y ha creado trabajos para gente como Riot Games, Wired Magazine, Youtube, BBC y The Atlantic, por nombrar algunos. Está enormemente inspirado por la cultura pop contemporánea en todas sus formas, desde películas, música, publicidad o deporte. La simplicidad es la clave de su trabajo, donde se esfuerza por reducir el nivel de detalle para permitir que la expresión de la idea reine de manera suprema.

DALE EDWIN MURRAY

www.daleedwinmurray.com
Instagram @demillustration
© pages 20

Dale Edwin Murray is a UK-based illustrator and graphic artist currently working out of his home studio in London. As well as producing commercial illustration commissions for the design, advertising and publishing industries, Dale also creates and sells his own graphic art prints.

Dale Edwin Murray es un ilustrador y artista gráfico del Reino Unido que actualmente trabaja en su estudio de Londres. Además de producir ilustraciones comerciales por encargo para industrias de diseño y publicidad, Dale también crea y vende sus propias obras de arte gráfico.

HARRY GRUNDMAN

www.harrymovieart.com
Instagram @grundmanis
Facebook @harry.grundmann
© pages 24, 80, 92

Riga based illustrator and graphic designer. He is better known as an artist in film industry, as he creates movie posters, concept art and storyboards. He also works on graphic design, where he is making visual material for brands. Harry gets most of his inspiration from movies from all around the world, particularly if they come from Asia. He is always excited about new projects, especially illustrations for books, animation or posters.

Ilustrador y diseñador gráfico, trabajando en Riga. Es más conocido como artista en la industria del cine por sus posters cinematográficos y storyboards. También trabaja en diseño gráfico, donde realiza material visual para marcas. Harry obtiene la mayor parte de su inspiración en películas de todo el mundo, particularmente del cine asiático. Siempre está entusiasmado con nuevos proyectos, especialmente si son ilustraciones para libros, animación o posters.

ORLANDO AROCENA

www.behance.net/orlandoarocena
Instagram @mexifunk
Twitter @OrlandoArocena
Facebook @orlandoarocenaillustrator
© pages 96

Orlando Arocena (Mexifunk) is an artist and graphic designer who works in traditional and digital mediums. After graduating from Pratt Institute, Brooklyn, NYC in 1994, he drew his way through Europe, co-founded Uptown Arts, and discovered he had a knack for digital commercial communications. He is also a dedicated member of the Poster Posse, a creative prolific international pop-culture group of artists who service the Hollywood Film Industry.

Orlando Arocena (Mexifunk) es un artista y diseñador gráfico que trabaja en medios tradicionales y digitales. Después de graduarse en el Pratt Institute, Brooklyn, Nueva York en 1994, se abrió camino en Europa, co-fundó Uptown Arts y descubrió que tenía una especial habilidad para las comunicaciones comerciales digitales. También es un miembro destacado de Poster Posse, un grupo de artistas creativos de la cultura pop internacional que trabajan para la industria cinematográfica de Hollywood.

IVAN SHAVRIN

www.artstation.com/shavrin_ivan
Instagram @ivan_shavrin_art
Facebook @shavrinart
© pages 88-89

Based in Siberia, he likes to say that this fact has no impact on his style, since the internet has made us all the same. His great passions are drawing and the cinematographic industry, considering Tarantino as one of the best directors of our time.

Afincado en Siberia, le gusta decir que este hecho no tiene ningún impacto en su estilo, ya que internet nos ha hecho iguales a todos. Sus grandes pasiones son el dibujo y la industria cinamatográfica, considerando a Tarantino como uno de los mejores directores de nuestro tiempo.

BOB DAHLSTROM

www.robertpfd.com
Instagram @Bobdahlstrom
Twitter @robertdahlstrom
© pages 98

Bob Dahlstrom lives in Illinois. He's married, has cats and draws a lot.

Bob Dahlstrom vive en Illinois. Está casado, le encantan los gatos y por supuesto dibujar mucho.

GERARDO LISANTI

www.gerardolisanti.it
Instagram @gerardo_lis
Facebook @lisantige
Twitter @lisantige
© pages 100

Gerardo is 28 years old and is an Italian graphic designer. His course of study has always developed in the artistic field. He graduated from art school and continued his studies at the Academy of Fine Arts in Rome. During his first work experiences, he mainly followed the development of brand images, the creation of logos and advertising campaigns for companies in various sectors. Gerardo currently work at Vertigo Cinema Creative Agency, a company that deals with the promotion and creation of film strategies, creating trailers, posters and social campaigns. The tribute to Quentin Tarantino that you find in these pages comes from the passion of the work he does and for that fantastic world called cinema.

Gerardo tiene 28 años y es un diseñador gráfico italiano. Su trayectoria siempre se ha desarrollado en el campo artístico, graduándose en la escuela de arte y continuando sus estudios en la Academia de Bellas Artes de Roma. Sus primeros trabajos, se centraron principalmente en imagen corporativa, creación de logotipos y campañas publicitarias para empresas de diversos sectores. Actualmente trabaja en Vertigo Cinema Creative Agency, una empresa que se ocupa de la promoción y creación de estrategias cinematográficas, creando trailers, carteles y campañas sociales. El homenaje a Quentin Tarantino que se encuentra en estas páginas proviene de la pasión por su trabajo, y por ese fantástico mundo llamado cine.

IBRAHEEM YOUSSEF

www.ibraheemyoussef.com
Instagram @ibraheemyoussef
© pages 21, 42, 44, 66

Ibraheem Youssef is an artist that is obsessed with pop culture. Having lived in three continents and multiple countries, he draws inspiration from many different cultures and places. His artwork has been featured and recognized by The Guardian, The Independent, Der Speigel, El Pais, Cannes, Communication Arts, Applied Arts to mention a few.

Ibraheem Youssef es un artista obsesionado con la cultura pop. Habiendo vivido en tres continentes y múltiples países, se inspira en muchas tradiciones y lugares diferentes. Su obra ha sido presentada y reconocida por The Guardian, The Independent, Der Speigel, El Pais, Cannes, Communication Arts, Applied Arts, entre otras.

RENATO CUNHA

www.renatoartes.wordpress.com
Instagram @renatodsc
Twitter @renatodscunha
Facebook @renatoartes
© pages 39

Renato Cunha is a freelance illustrator, born in Belém do Pará, but raised in Santos, São Paulo. He started as most illustrators begin: drawing superheroes and copying comics. He has lent his talent to brands such as Nerdstore, Itubaína, Dove Men Care, Rolling Stone Magazine, Copag, Mahogany and WBeer Magazine. Although Renato almost always uses the computer in his creations, he has never abandoned the good old pencil and paper. His influences range from Pop Art to Surrealism, to comic books and even to tattoos.

Renato Cunha es un ilustrador independiente, nacido en Belém do Pará, pero criado en Santos, São Paulo. Comenzó como la mayoría de los ilustradores comienzan: dibujando superhéroes y copiando cómics. Ha prestado su talento a marcas como Nerdstore, Itubaína, Dove Men Care, Rolling Stone Magazine, Copag, Mahogany y WBeer Magazine. Aunque Renato casi siempre usa medios digitales en sus creaciones, nunca ha abandonado el lápiz y el papel. Sus influencias van desde el arte pop o el surrealismo, hasta los cómics e incluso los tatuajes.

MARÍA SUÁREZ-INCLÁN

www.msinclan.com
Instagram @m_sinclan
Facebook @msinclan
© pages 2-3

María Suárez-Inclán is a spanish multidisciplinar creative Graphic designer and Illustrator based in London, UK. She graduated in Graphic Design at Universidad Complutense of Madrid, and also studied simultaneously Psychology at the same university.
Since she remembers, María has always been interested in Art and loved drawing. Besides Illustration and Graphic design, she is also passionate about comic books, film, art and people.

María Suárez-Inclán es una diseñadora gráfica e ilustradora multidisciplinar española con sede en Londres, Reino Unido. Se graduó en Diseño Gráfico en la Universidad Complutense de Madrid y también estudió Psicología en la misma universidad.
Desde que recuerda, a María siempre le ha interesado el arte y el dibujo. Además de la ilustración y diseño gráfico, también le apasionan los cómics, el cine, el arte y la gente.

KREG FRANCO

www.kregfranco.com
Instagram @kregfranco
Twitter @kregfranco
Facebook @kregfrancoartcollection
© pages 43

He seeks to capture the essence of people and characters through portraits. He is constantly enriching his knowledge through observations, illustrating portraits in diverse ways according to the subject. Kreg is a NYC-based illustrator and tattoo artist who obtained a BFA in Illustration from the Fashion Institute of Technology, and he is graduate of the High School of Art & Design. He is currently tattooing and illustrating at East Side Ink. His goal is to have viewers recognize the soul in his portraits, as each face has its own story to tell. What sort of story would you tell in yours?

Busca capturar la esencia de las personas y los personajes a través de los retratos. Constantemente está enriqueciendo su conocimiento a través de observaciones, ilustrando retratos de diversas maneras según el tema. Kreg es un ilustrador y artista de tatuajes afincado en Nueva York que obtuvo un BFA en Ilustración del Fashion Institute of Technology, y se graduó en la High School of Art & Design. Actualmente se encuentra tatuando e ilustrando en East Side Ink. Su objetivo es que los espectadores reconozcan el alma en sus retratos, ya que cada rostro tiene su propia historia que contar. ¿Qué tipo de historia contarías en la tuya?

JULIAN RENTZSCH

www.julianrentzsch.de
www.stellavie.com
Instagram @julianrentzsch
Instagram @stellavie.hamburg
© pages 11

Julian Rentzsch has been working as a freelance illustrator for customers, publishers and agencies worldwide since 2009.
Stellavie is an independent and creatively led graphic design and printmaking studio from Hamburg, Germany.

Julian Rentzsch ha trabajado como ilustrador independiente para clientes, editores y agencias en todo el mundo desde 2009.
Stellavie es un estudio independiente y creativo de diseño gráfico y estampación de Hamburgo, Alemania.

WAYNE MAGUIRE

Instagram @Inkedikons
Facebook @inkedikons
© pages 78-79, 90

Wayne Maguire is an Irish freelance artist. His work is a mixture of his love for movies and tattoo culture. His INKED IKONS collection is an example of this, where he has taken some of his favorite actors and characters and added relevant tattoos. All of Wayne's work is hand drawn with pencils.

Wayne Maguire es un artista independiente irlandés. Su trabajo es una mezcla de su amor por el cine y la cultura del tatuaje. Su colección INKED IKONS es un buen ejemplo, dibuja a sus actores y personajes favoritos, agregándoles tatuajes. Todo su trabajo está hecho a mano con lápiz.

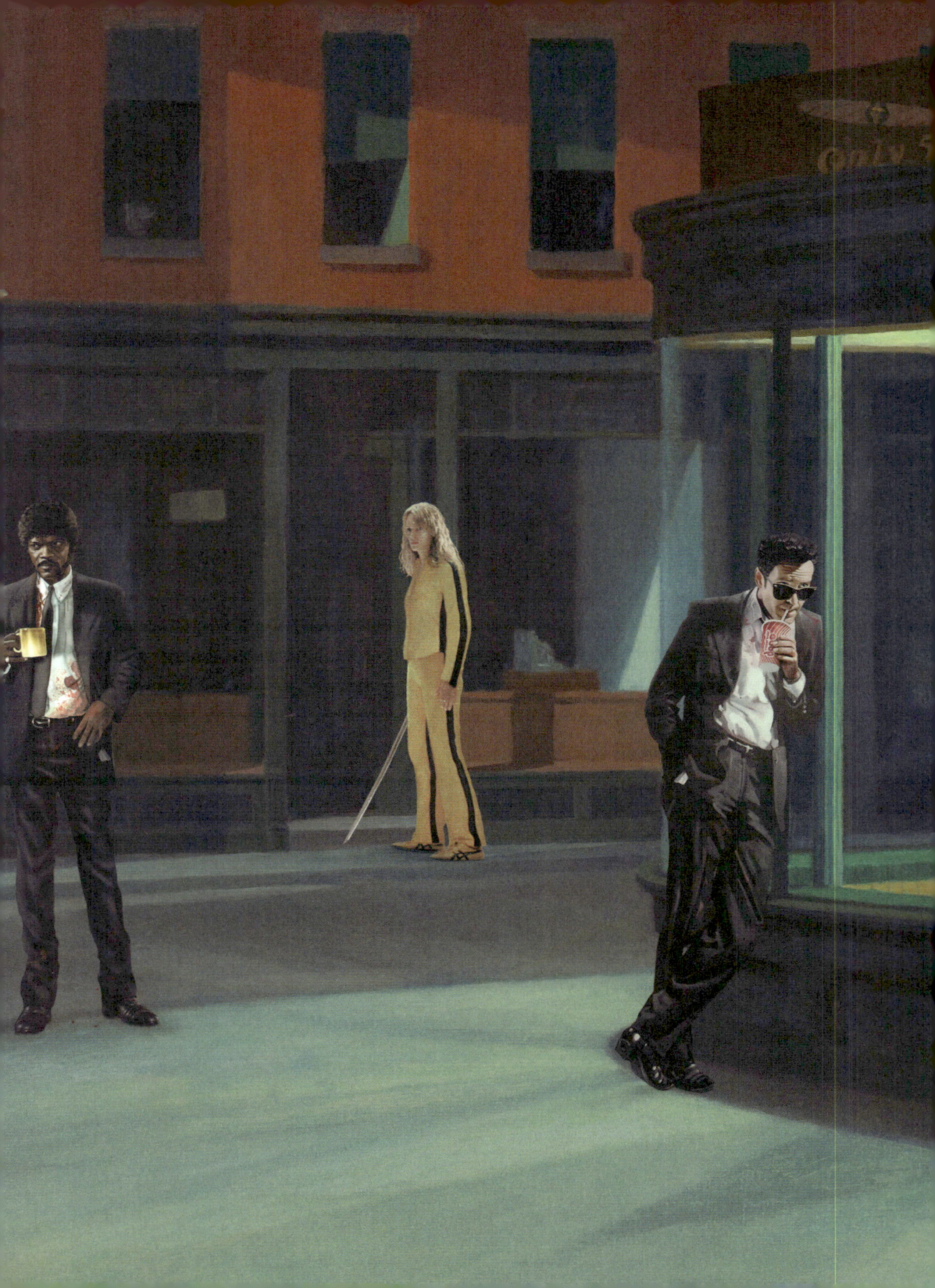
Only